The Visual Dictionary of Illustration

An AVA Book
Published by AVA Publishing SA
Rue des Fontenailles 16
Case Postale
1000 Lausanne 6
Switzerland
Tel: +41 786 005 109
Email: enquiries@avabooks.ch

Distributed by Thames & Hudson (ex-North America)
181a High Holborn
London WC1V 7QX
United Kingdom
Tel: +44 20 7845 5000
Fax: +44 20 7845 5055
Email: sales@thameshudson.co.uk
www.thamesandhudson.com

Distributed in the USA & Canada by
Ingram Publisher Services Inc.
1 Ingram Blvd.
La Vergne, TN 37086
USA
Tel: +1 866 400 5351
Fax: +1 800 838 1149
Email: customer.service@ingrampublisherservices.com
www.ingrampublisherservices.com

English Language Support Office
AVA Publishing (UK) Ltd.
Tel: +44 1903 204 455
Email: enquiries@avabooks.ch

ISBN 978-2-940373-90-1

10 9 8 7 6 5 4 3 2 1

Design by Gavin Ambrose
www.gavinambrose.co.uk

Production by AVA Book Production Pte. Ltd.,
Singapore
Tel: +65 6334 8173
Fax: +65 6259 9830
Email: production@avabooks.com.sg

All reasonable attempts have been made to trace, clear and
credit the copyright holders of the images reproduced in this
book. However, if any credits have been inadvertently
omitted, the publisher will endeavour to incorporate
amendments in future editions.

The Visual Dictionary
of Illustration

How to get the most out of this book   4

This book is an easy-to-use reference to the key terms used in illustration. Each entry comprises a brief textual definition along with a drawing or visual example of the point under discussion. Supplementary contextual information is also included.

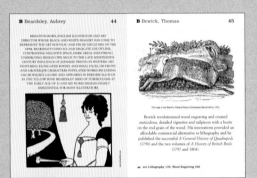

Key areas addressed in this book are those terms commonly used in reference to the study of illustration.

Entries are presented in alphabetical order to provide an easy reference system.

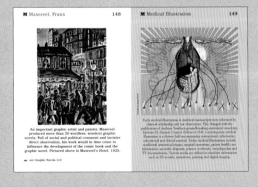

A unique print often created by placing paper on artwork that is produced on a metal plate or glass, and then printing via an etching or litho press. Variations are created depending on how the plate is inked. Mono prints can be created in many ways including collage, hand-colouring, working directly on to a screen and forcing the ink through with a squeegee. The image below is a mono print by Ceri Amphlett.

Decorative images constructed from small cubes of coloured stone, ceramic, glass or marble. Mosaics were used extensively by the Romans for floor and wall decorations. Religious themes are portrayed in outstanding examples by Byzantine artists of mosaic in Constantinople (now Istanbul). The image above is of a mosaic by Jane Sybilla Fordham.

☞ see Vienna Secession 252

Each page contains a single entry and, where appropriate, a printer's hand symbol ☞ provides page references to other related and relevant entries.

A timeline helps to provide historical context for selected key moments in the development and evolution of illustration.

Introduction

Welcome to *The Visual Dictionary of Illustration*, a book
that provides textual definitions and visual explanations
for common terms found in the key areas of illustration
and pertinent entries from related arts.

This book aims to provide clear definitions to the
myriad of terms used within illustration. It includes
explanations of commonly misused terms; the difference
between *doodles* and *drawings* or *ornithological*
and *conceptual* illustrations; and the significance of
key figures in the world of illustration. *The Visual
Dictionary of Illustration* provides visual explanations
from the traditional and the classic, to the contemporary
and experimental.

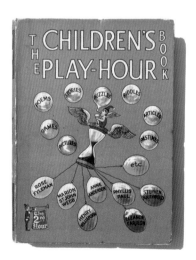

Facing page: This piece was created for
an indoor campaign for a vintage clothes
shop (Art and design by Jose Palma at
La Oveja Negra).

Left: *The Children's Play-Hour Book* from
the author's collection. It is illustrated with
colour plates and published by Longmans,
Green and Co Ltd in 1928.

Facing page (left):
This figurative illustration of
New York is by Camberwell
College of Arts, London
graduate, Chris Dent.

Facing page (right): This
illustration is from the
large-format, contemporary
graphic art magazine
Le Gun produced by
graduates from the Royal
College of Arts, London.

Left: This teddy bear
illustration was created
by Ceri Amphlett.

*teddies who love
life itself*

Illustrations visually communicate content for reproduction in imaginative, distinctive and highly personal ways while solving problems, decorating, entertaining, adorning, commenting, informing, inspiring, explaining, educating, provoking, beguiling, enchanting and storytelling.

A clear understanding of the key terms used in illustration will help you to better articulate and formalise your ideas, and will ensure greater accuracy in the transfer of those ideas to others.

The field of illustration is flourishing and it is now a powerful, vibrant and constantly evolving and expanding applied art form. It is an ancient medium with a rich history; it is also a vital, dynamic and contemporary means of expression, interpretation and communication, which conveys ideas and messages with compelling imagery created in any media.

The following text provides thought-provoking, compact and basic definitions of terminology and instructive insights into categories of illustration, important fundamental principles, methods, materials, equipment, technical advances, techniques and movements in art and design that are associated with illustration. A broad and contextual approach to the field draws links, cross-references and parallels between entries and is supplemented by visual explanations that elucidate and expand on the key terms.

The book also includes a timeline charting the evolution of, and developments within, the field of illustration and covers works by artists such as Albrecht Dürer, Jacques Callot, William Hogarth, Goya and Honoré Daumier.

Facing page:
This is illustrator Annabel Hudson holding one of her creations.

Left: Illustration by Andy Potts, demonstrating the varied and eclectic nature of the modern illustrator. The illustration uses a myriad of techniques and styles to create a single, cohesive style.

Andy Potts

Contents

The Dictionary

A term denoting visual art characterised by formalised qualities and non-representational forms. In painting, abstract refers to historical styles of non-objective or gestural paintings.

The creation of images that amplify texts and embrace the ridiculous and irrational. Historical examples include Edward Lear's *Book of Nonsense* (1846), and Sir John Tenniel's illustrations for *Alice's Adventures in Wonderland* (1865). Dada and Surrealism set out to shock the middle classes with work that was contrary to reason. In 1934, illustrator W. Heath Robinson used the title 'Absurdities' to describe a collection of his exuberant and humorous drawings.

This was a promotional piece created for *Ware* magazine in answer to a brief to create an abstract image around power and strength in sport.

Illustration by Andy Potts

☞ see Narrative 156, Tenniel, Sir John 232

'Plankton People' painted in liquitex acrylic by Mark Wigan

A quick-drying paint with pigments,
mixed with synthetic resin. Acrylics can be used with
other media to create a thick impasto effect.

A creative and commercial field that provides more exposure and pays more than most commissions. Deadlines are short within the industry and the collaboration between agents, art buyers, designers, art directors and copywriters is essential in order to effectively communicate the client's message. Illustrators bring personal vision, drawing and design skills, wit, creative imagination and interpretive skills to the task.

Illustration by Andy Potts

This was the main brand illustration and guide cover for the Proms 2008 festival.

A person or organisation
formally authorised to represent
the illustrator to prospective
clients. Agents promote artists
and secure commissions for
them by using their portfolios.
They conduct business
transactions with a client on
behalf of the illustrator. The
illustrator then pays the agent a
fee or commission in exchange
for securing clients and
promoting his or her work.

☞ see Commission 68

PECK'S ARCADE,
207, 209 & 211 Broadway,
Opp. Mansion House.

This is an allegorical Victorian souvenir card showing an ambiguous narrative as the couple runs away, only to be faced by an oncoming train.

A form of extended metaphor used to describe a narrative that does not serve to provide a literal interpretation. This gives a story an underlying symbolic meaning, where characters can become personifications of ideas. Allegorical tales that have inspired acclaimed illustrations include *Aesop's fables*, Dante Alighieri's *The Divine Comedy*, George Orwell's *Animal Farm* and William Golding's *Lord of the Flies*.

☞ see Personification 170

These books were first published during the late eighteenth century, and were mostly illustrated with vignettes. The illustrations elucidated a wide variety of subjects including allegories, myths, scenes from everyday life, science, humour and satire. Examples include the prolific output of German illustrator Daniel Chodowiecki and calendars such as the Göttinger Taschenkalender in 1778.

☞ see Vignettes 253

Publications designed to help children learn the alphabet.
The letters are often complemented by narrative illustrations.
Alphabet books developed from early instructional religious
and secular moral texts, hornbook wooden tablets and printed
battledores. The ABC format was utilised for primers and
spellers, which featured rhyming couplets and woodcuts.

The above images were designed for an oversized, interactive alphabet game. The brief called for
realistic animals that also had a warm and friendly feel.

☞ see Typography 244

The alternative comics publishing industry is a descendant of the small press of the 1960s and the 1970s underground comic and publications. Contemporary publishers at the forefront of the field include *Fantagraphics, Drawn and Quarterly, Top Shelf* and *High Water*. The field also includes a large DIY community of mini-comics, web comics and zine makers.

Illustrations from *Spooky Tales* by Isabel Samaras and Gary Panter

☞ see Blab! 46, Comics 66, Kramers Ergot 134

DEALS WITH THE REPRESENTATION OF PEOPLE EITHER OBJECTIVELY OR IN A STYLISED WAY BY STUDYING AND DEMONSTRATING A KNOWLEDGE OF THE STRUCTURE OF THE HUMAN BODY. THE RENAISSANCE INSPIRED ARTISTS WITH NEW IDEAS AND A FOCUS ON HUMANITY AND NATURALISM, USING DIRECT OBSERVATION, PRECISE INVESTIGATION AND THE INTRODUCTION OF PERSPECTIVE. THE DETAILED VISUAL ANALYSIS OF THE STRUCTURE OF THE BODY IS EVIDENT IN THE NOTEBOOKS OF LEONARDO DA VINCI, DRAWINGS OF ALBRECHT DÜRER AND MICHELANGELO'S SISTINE CHAPEL CEILING.

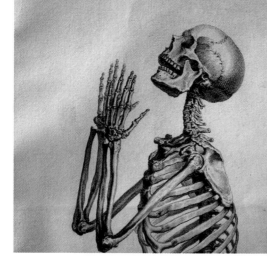

☞ see Life Drawing 136, Observational Drawing 160, Renaissance 195

The optical illusion of movement employed through persistence of vision. Animator Norman McLaren stated that 'animation is not the art of drawings that move, but the art of movements that are drawn'. The field developed in the early nineteenth century with optical devices such as the thaumatrope and zoetrope. Techniques employed in animation include: 2D, 3D, claymation, paint on glass, stop motion, silhouettes, pin screen and digitally-filmed, interpolated, rotoscoped animations.

The following animation sequence was art directed by Richard Higgs from Big Squid and the animation was produced by Chris Gledhill, Visual Effects Director at GraphixAsset Ltd.

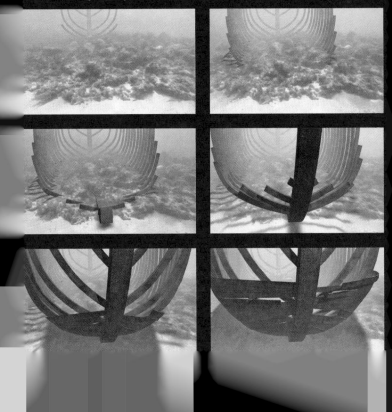

Commercial source books used by illustrators for promotion. These are distributed to art directors, art buyers and designers. Artwork is also entered for competition in annuals and judged by peers.

List of annuals:
Contact
Creative Handbook
The Artbook
3x3 Illustration Directory
Image
The Black Book
Image, The Directory of Illustration
BIG
The I-Spot
Workbook
Le Book
Children's Illustrators.com
Swedish Illustrators' Workbook
Images AOI
D&AD Annual
Creative Review Annual
Society of Illustrators' Annual
American Illustration
Lüerzer's 200 Best Illustrators Worldwide
3x3 Eyes, Bologna
Communication Arts
Illustration File Japan
The Big Book of Illustration

☞ see Organisations 161, Self Promotion 208

Inflatable character by Devil Robots

The bestowing of human characteristics or traits on animals or objects. This is employed in fables, fairy tales and children's books such as Charles H Bennett's interpretation of *Aesop's Fables*; Sir John Tenniel's illustrations for Lewis Carroll's *Alice in Wonderland*; AB Frost's *Uncle Remus*; Ernest H Shepard's illustrations for *The Wind in the Willows* and Beatrix Potter's *The Tale of Peter Rabbit*.

☞ see Potter, Beatrix 185, Tenniel, Sir John 232

IN ILLUSTRATION, APPROPRIATION IS THE CONSCIOUS AND INTENTIONAL BORROWING OF ELEMENTS AND TECHNIQUES OF OTHER ARTISTS' AND ILLUSTRATORS' WORK. PLAGIARISM HAS ALWAYS BEEN PREVALENT IN ILLUSTRATION – SOME ILLUSTRATORS MAKE A LIVING BY SIMPLY IMITATING THE STYLE OF ANOTHER ARTIST OR ILLUSTRATOR. REFERENCE MATERIAL COULD ALSO BE REWORKED AND SIGNIFICANTLY TRANSFORMED BY ILLUSTRATORS IN THEIR OWN PIECES. MANY ARTISTS, SUCH AS ANDY WARHOL, ROY LICHTENSTEIN, JEFF KOONS AND DAMIEN HIRST, HAVE BORROWED FROM COMMERCIAL ARTISTS' WORK – TRANSFORMING LOW ART INTO SUPPOSEDLY HIGH ART. QUESTIONS OVER INTELLECTUAL PROPERTY, COPYRIGHT, NEW MEANINGS AND ORIGINALITY ARE ALL ASPECTS THAT COME WITH THIS TERRITORY.

☞ see Style 226

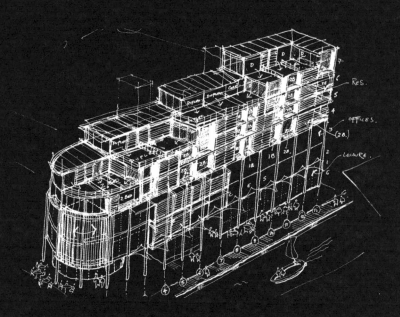

Detailed artwork created through the use of traditional
or digital techniques by professional illustrators to
present a proposed architectural construction, interior
space, landscape setting or floor and site plans. These
drawings are produced to assist architects, designers
and planners.

The above drawing was Cartwright Pickard Architects' proposal for a sustainable office
development in York city centre, UK

see Drawing 86, Observational Drawing 160

A store or repository of images, documents or compressed computer files that can act as a directory of visual information for the illustrator's future use. Many illustrators build and preserve their own special collection of inspirational visual material for reference purposes.

A POPULAR AND ECLECTIC, INTERNATIONAL, DECORATIVE DESIGN AND ARCHITECTURAL MOVEMENT POPULAR IN THE 1920s AND 1930s. IT IS CHARACTERISED BY STREAMLINED SHARP LINES, ZIGZAGS, GEOMETRIC FORMS AND MOTIFS AND THE USE OF MATERIALS SUCH AS PLASTICS, CHROME AND GLASS. THE DISTINCTIVE FEATURES OF ART DECO ALSO AFFECTED INTERIOR DESIGN, HOME FURNISHINGS AND ILLUSTRATIONS, FROM BOOK JACKETS AND ADVERTISING POSTERS TO FASHION DRAWINGS AND STAGE SET DESIGNS.

These covers are from 1930s illustrated McCall fashion catalogues from the author's collection.

☞ see Book Jacket 49

A term that covers a variety of positions in publishing, film, television, advertising and video game production. The art director's role in publishing is to work with editors and oversee, select and supervise all the editorial artwork and production for a magazine, book or website, including aspects such as photography, graphic design and illustration. In advertising, art directors work with copywriters to generate concepts and oversee the visual appearance and production of campaigns.

The above are images of experiments in hand-cut montage for a London-based bar and restaurant, which changed décor seasonally. The designs were created by Studio Output.

☞ see Campaign 55, Collage 64, Graphic Design 109

This term means 'new art' in French, and it is called *jugendstil* or 'youth style' in Germany. Art Nouveau was an international movement and decorative style in art, architecture, consumer products, fashion and graphics, popular from 1890 to the early 1900s. It contributed to the break with nineteenth-century neoclassical historicism and the transition to twentieth-century modernism. Distinctive organic motifs, whiplash curves, asymmetrical letterforms, arabesques and undulating lines are characteristic of this movement, and these traits are evident in the chromolithographic posters of Jules Chéret, Eugene Grasset and Alphonse Mucha.

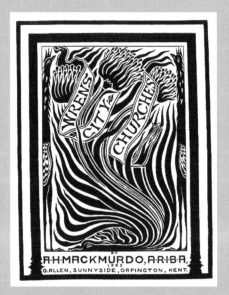

This is Arthur Mackmurdo's title page for *Wren's City Churches* (1883), woodcut on paper.

☞ see Style 226, Woodcut 265

A LATE-NINETEENTH CENTURY DECORATIVE ARTS, DESIGN AND ARCHITECTURAL MOVEMENT THAT ORIGINATED IN BRITAIN TO PROMOTE QUALITY DESIGN AND IMPROVE PEOPLE'S LIVES. IT EMERGED IN RESPONSE TO THE EFFECTS OF THE POOR DESIGN OF THE INDUSTRIAL REVOLUTION. THE MOVEMENT WAS INSPIRED BY JOHN RUSKIN AND WILLIAM MORRIS. THE ARTS AND CRAFTS MOVEMENT LED TO THE ESTABLISHMENT OF THE PRIVATE PRESS MOVEMENT. THIS FONT IS BASED ON THE WORKS OF CHARLES RENNIE MACKINTOSH.

A fanciful William Morris illustration by Mario Hugo; graphite on a torn book page can be seen in Shadrach Lindo's *Cavalier* book and the Nog Gallery, London.

☞ see Graphic Design 109

A school that specialises in the study of visual arts such as painting, drawing, sculpture, ceramics, illustration, graphic design, photography and digital media. Students create imaginative work while acquiring knowledge, intellectual and practical skills.

☞ see Sketchbook 215

Work produced by fitting pieces together, often making use of unrelated or found objects. Assemblage reflects the ritual artefacts, shrines and costumes of primitive societies, the inventive worlds of visionary art and the fragmentary experience of modern civilisation. It is a tradition evident in Dada, Surrealism, Pop Art and Postmodernism. Some illustrators specialise in constructing three-dimensional assemblages and photographing them for published contexts.

This is one of a series of heads created by Camberwell College of Arts illustration graduate, Mark Hadley for his degree show in 2008.

THE ACT OF TAKING
RESPONSIBILITY FOR
ORIGINATING OR INITIATING
IDEAS FOR LITERARY, MUSICAL
OR ILLUSTRATIVE WORKS.
AUTHORIAL PRACTICE THROUGH
SELF-INITIATED AND
INDEPENDENT PROJECTS IN THE
SEQUENTIAL AND NARRATIVE
FIELDS GIVES ILLUSTRATORS
GREATER AUTONOMY. THESE
AREAS CAN ENCOMPASS
CHILDREN'S BOOKS, COMICS,
GRAPHIC NOVELS, VISUAL
ESSAYS AND ANIMATIONS.

see Children's Books 61, Narrative 156

In French, this term means 'vanguard', or 'advance guard' – a term applied to art that challenges the accepted status quo, commercial values and conventions. This was seen as a key trait of modernism and was dismissed as a redundant way of thinking by postmodernist theorists.

The mannerisms and styles of avant-garde art movements, such as Futurism, Cubism, Dada, Surrealism, Fluxus, COBRA, Abstract Expressionism, Mail Art and Pop Art, borrowed images from commercial art. These styles have often been appropriated in turn by illustrators and designers for the sale of commodities within mass consumer culture.

A device or emblem, such as a woven patch, embroidered symbol or metal button, which can function as a form of identification, indicate membership of a group or denote an award or rank. It is a small, witty and collectable object used for promotional and advertising purposes to express a cultural allegiance. Button badges were first produced in the 1890s and, like the T-shirt, have been associated with political protest and youth culture.

☞ see T-shirt 243

THIS TAPESTRY IS APPROXIMATELY 50CM WIDE BY 71M LONG. IT IS A PRECURSOR OF THE COMIC BOOK OR STORYBOARD, AND IS AN IMPORTANT EXAMPLE OF SEQUENTIAL GRAPHIC STORYTELLING. ITS PICTORIAL NARRATIVE DEPICTS THE BUILD-UP TO AND THE INVASION OF ENGLAND BY THE NORMANS IN 1066. THE EXACT ORIGINS AND HISTORY OF THIS FAMILIAR AND ICONIC ARTEFACT REMAIN HIGHLY DISPUTED.

This is a detail from the eleventh-century woven Bayeux Tapestry.

☞ see Storyboard 222

BRIGHTON-BORN, ENGLISH ILLUSTRATOR AND ART DIRECTOR WHOSE BLACK-AND-WHITE IMAGERY HAS COME TO REPRESENT THE ART NOUVEAU AND FIN DE SIÈCLE ERA OF THE 1890s. BEARDSLEY'S SINUOUS AND DELICATE USE OF LINE, CONTRASTING NEGATIVE SPACE, DARK AREAS AND STRONG UNDERLYING DESIGN OWE MUCH TO THE LATE NINETEENTH-CENTURY INFLUENCE OF JAPANESE PRINTS ON WESTERN ART. FEATURING ELONGATED BODIES AND SMALL FACES, HIS EROTIC AND GROTESQUE CHARACTERS POPULATED WORKS INCLUDING OSCAR WILDE'S *SALOME* AND APPEARED IN PERIODICALS SUCH AS *THE YELLOW BOOK*. BEARDSLEY DIED OF TUBERCULOSIS AT THE EARLY AGE OF 25 AND HIS WORKS REMAIN HIGHLY INFLUENTIAL FOR MANY ILLUSTRATORS.

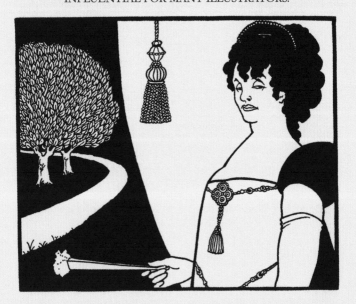

This image is from Bewick's *A General History of Quadrupeds* (Second edition, 1791).

Bewick revolutionised wood engraving and created meticulous, detailed vignettes and tailpieces with a burin on the end-grain of the wood. His innovations provided an affordable commercial alternative to lithography and he published the successful *A General History of Quadrupeds* (1790) and the two volumes of *A History of British Birds* (1797 and 1804).

see Lithography 139, Wood Engraving 266

A publication featuring fine art, illustration and comic work by leading contemporary image-makers. Edited by Monte Beauchamp and initially published by Kitchen Sink Press, Blab! is now an annual coffee-table showcase published by Fantagraphics. Lowbrow and alternative comic book artists who have adorned its pages include: Gary Baseman, Shag, Tim Biskup, Gary Panter, Mark Ryden, Sue Coe, Joe Coleman, Camille Rose Garcia, Daniel Clowes, Spain Rodriguez and Kim Deitch.

The influential and idiosyncratic British artist and poet, who was inspired by the Bible, his own religious visions and the revolutionary ideas he fostered in his imaginative mythological world. His family were dissenters and he was opposed to slavery, racism and sexual inequality. Blake developed the relief-etching process, or 'illuminated printing', to produce books such as *Songs of Innocence and Experience*, *The Marriage of Heaven and Hell* and *Jerusalem*. These works are often cited as the forerunners to graphic novels and artists' books.

☞ see Book Art 48, Livre d'artiste 141

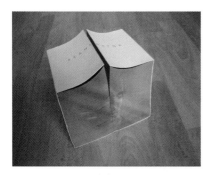

Book art generally involves projects that engage with the conventions of book production. Pictorial and textual elements, materials and structure are manipulated to express the artists' ideas, and the form of the book or book-like object often aligns with its content. The genre is becoming a popular area of expression for both contemporary illustrators and artists.

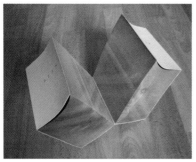

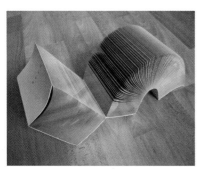

Matt Lumby's *Reanimator* book utilises edge-to-edge colour printing to reveal an image on the book's edges. The book has two spines and the page block is cleaved in two. The image effect is achieved by dividing the original image into single lines of horizontal pixels, and then stretching the pixels to fill the book's pages to both edges.

the double shuffle

james hadley chase

*The wrapper around a hardcover book, which protects
the volume from dust and light. They could also
function as small, promotional posters for advertising
a book. From the 1920s and the introduction of
lithography, the pictorial jacket has evoked mood and
atmosphere through the use of visual metaphors.
Exemplars in this field include Edward McKnight
Kauffer for Random House, Deutscher Taschenbuch
Verlag and the witty cover art of Penguin books.*

☞ see Book Art 48

Highly detailed and scientifically accurate drawings,
engravings or watercolour paintings that depict the
distinguishing features, colours and details of plant
species. Botanical illustration has a long history. It
emerged in order to assist the scientific study of plants
and to identify their medicinal, edible and poisonous
properties. This field developed from painted, early
sixth-century herbal manuscripts to sixteenth-century
woodcuts and eventually, lavishly printed books.

☞ see Herbals 114, Potter, Beatrix 185

The process of solving problems by generating lists of key
words and ideas. Ilustrators can make lists of words, image
associations, visual metaphors and similes that are related to a
brief. Thoughts and ideas can be made tangible by generating
thumbnail sketches, creating links and juxtapositions, adding
new twists, introducing design principles and utilising spider
diagrams and mindmaps.

Spider diagrams

An intuitive visual language that forms a spider-like shape, combining Venn diagrams and
Euler circles to express sets of relations.

Mindmaps

Developed by Tony Buzan in the 1960s to explore connections and relationships
between ideas and words.

This school was founded in the 1900s by the father of American illustration, Howard Pyle, at Chadds Ford, Pennsylvania. He wanted to promote his figurative vision of American art and stated that his aim in teaching 'will not be the production of book illustrators, but rather the production of painters of pictures'. His students trained in picture-making, staging scenes and composition, and were encouraged to project themselves into the subject matter and live in their pictures. His students included NC Wyeth, Jessie Wilcox Smith and Frank Schoonover.

This is a Howard Pyle illustration from the *Book of Pirates*.

Illustration by Andy Potts

Concise and detailed preparatory instructions given to the illustrator providing relevant information on the objective of the commission. In the highly competitive world of illustration, the ability to interpret the brief is as fundamental as convincing drawing, strong ideas and design skills. Deadlines are usually tight and must be adhered to. Research and immersion in the subject matter are also required in order to pitch the message effectively to a target audience.

The illustration above is one of 11 created for Italian company Carraro's 2007 annual report.

Formal
Briefs that adhere to established conventions and standards used in visual communication projects.

Informal
Briefs that are casual, unofficial or verbal.

☞ see Research 198

Highly influential nineteenth-century British illustrator, who produced toy books for the colour printer and engraver, Edmund Evans. His work was admired for convincing draughtsmanship, economy of line and colour, the balance of compositions and detail. Caldecott's work conveyed wit, charm and humour, often depicting huntsmen, dogs, horses and Georgian costumed characters in pastel colours. The Caldecott Medal awarded for children's book illustration was named after him.

NOT SUCH DISAGREEABLE WEATHER FOR THE HAYMAKERS
AS SOME PEOPLE THINK.

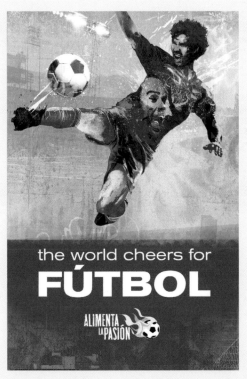

the world cheers for
FÚTBOL
ALIMENTA LA PASIÓN

This image was used to promote soccer in McDonald's stores across Latin America.

A comprehensive and integrated strategy that utilises a series of messages based on a theme and uses a variety of media such as web, broadcast, ambient and print.

☞ see Advertising 21

JOHN BULL taking a Luncheon: — or — British Cooks, cramming Old Grumble-Gizzard, with Bonne-Chère.

From the Italian *caricare* meaning 'to load or charge', caricature is representation based on the distortion, exaggeration and over-emphasis of a person's distinctive characteristics. Often satirical and insulting, they can mock and make people appear ridiculous. Exemplars include Thomas Rowlandson, James Gillray, George Cruikshank and Honoré Daumier.

☞ see Cartoon 57, Satire 202

Before the nineteenth century, this term referred to a full-size preparatory drawing used to plan a fresco, mosaic, mural, tapestry, window or carpet. The term now also denotes a humorous or satirical drawing found in newspapers and magazines, often commenting on topical events; a sequential comic strip or animation.

☞ see Humour 118, Punch 189

A SMALL, POCKET-SIZED, CHEAPLY PRODUCED BOOK FEATURING EVERYTHING FROM NURSERY RHYMES, BAWDY STORIES, RELIGIOUS TRACTS, BALLADS, POETRY, HUMOROUS AND MORAL TALES, TRAGEDIES, LOVE STORIES AND ADVENTURES. FROM THE 1570S TO THE 1850S, THEY WERE SOLD IN BOXES CARRIED BY ITINERANT PEDDLERS KNOWN AS 'CHAPMEN', THE NAME DERIVED FROM THE ANGLO SAXON WORD, MEANING 'TO SELL, BARTER OR TRADE'. CHAPBOOKS WERE PRINTED AND DISTRIBUTED IN SOUTH AMERICA AND MEXICO UNTIL THE LATE 1930S. THE SPIRIT OF CHAPBOOKS CONTINUES TODAY IN THE FORM OF POETRY CHAPBOOKS, ZINES, ALTERNATIVE COMICS, ARTISTS' BOOKS AND ONLINE BLOGGING.

Gymnastics

Basketball

Fencing

Karate

Athletics

Cycling

Canoeing

Rugby

Tennis

Illustration by Rafa Ruiz at La Oveja Negra

An illustration that possesses features and human attributes in order to portray believable roles in narratives, such as graphic novels, children's books, computer games and animated films.

The images above are characterisations of some of the sporting events held during the summer Olympics.

☛ see Children's Books 61

Image by Mireille Fauchon

A term that originates from the Italian for 'clear, bright' *(chiaro)* and 'dark, obscure' *(oscuro)*. It is used to describe the treatment of contrasts between dark and light in an image. During the Renaissance, artists produced chiaroscuro drawings using the dark base of coloured paper and ink, highlighting with white gouache. Light modelling or shading has been used in painting since the Middle Ages. Exponents of the strong use of chiaroscuro include Caravaggio, Rembrandt, the film-maker Sergei Eisenstein and contemporary graphic artist, Frank Miller.

☞ see Life Drawing 136, Observational Drawing 160

C Children's Books

Books intended to be read by people under the age of 18. The genre includes a wide variety of works from picture books, comics, non-fiction, literary classics, periodicals, fairy stories, folklore and fables. Many children's books contain a moral. They visually entertain and instruct through illustrations as well as texts. Successful children's books create believable worlds with original and exciting images. They employ a bold use of colour, contain strong ideas, consistent characterisation and intelligent designs that all combine to engage the child's imagination.

Illustrations in children's books can be enchanting, strange and dark, as seen in this work by Camberwell College of Arts MA graduate, Subin Lee.

☞ see Alphabet Books 25

Illustration by Alex Robbins

An individual or an organisation that pays for receiving the professional services of a freelance illustrator and/or illustration agency.

☞ see Agent 22, Commission 68

The act of working with others to create something. Collaboration is an important aspect of professional illustration. An illustrator is likely to collaborate with agents, art directors, editors, art buyers, designers, publishers, gallery directors and clients. Communication and presentation skills are, therefore, vital talents to develop. Increasingly, illustrators and designers are forming their own multidisciplinary collectives in order to obtain and exert greater creative control.

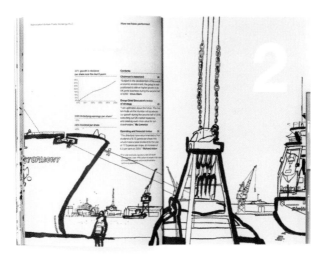

The client for this project (ABP) required a solution that would capture both the attention and imagination of investors, which communicated the business's positive, competitive edge. The illustrator, Lucinda Rogers, was commissioned to produce a series of reportage sketches that reflect the busy, bustling atmosphere of a port and thus, of the client's business. The project was designed by NB Studio.

☞ see Art Director 35

Derived from the French word *coller* meaning 'to glue or stick'.
Collage is the arranging and creating of a new image by using
various materials. The technique dates back to ancient
civilisations and was used for communicative, ritual and
decorative purposes. Collage was used in China upon the
invention of paper; for calligraphy in tenth-century Japan; in
the religious icons of medieval Europe; and for popular
scrapbooks and albums in nineteenth-century Britain. Notable
artists who have utilised collage include Pablo Picasso and
Henri Matisse.

This example by José Palma at La Oveja Negra uses mixed media.

Objects produce different sensations in the eye due to the way they emit or reflect light. The use of colour intensifies psychological and emotional responses in the viewer, heightens perception and provides cultural and symbolic associations; some examples are shown below.

Scarlet red: Exciting, dynamic, dramatic and aggressive.

Magenta: Passionate, flamboyant and attention grabbing.

Orange: Fun, glowing and vital – the warmest of colours.

Bright yellow: Hopeful and cheery, but also cowardly and deceitful.

Chocolate: Succulent, durable and delicious.

Lilac: Feminine, refined, elegant and graceful.

Lavender: Floral, nostalgic and eccentric.

Purple: Sensual, futuristic and embracing.

Plum: Full-bodied, plump, sophisticated and unique.

Electric blue: Dynamic, engaging, bold and exhilarating.

Navy: Reliable, safe, traditional and constant.

Baby blue: Cute, youthful, serene, quiet, cosy and subdued.

Dark green: Natural, organic, plentiful and luscious.

Black: Magical, dramatic, elegant, sinister and bold.

White: Pure, innocent, good and clinical.

Gold: Wealthy, extravagant, excessive, lucky and traditional.

Silver: Prestigious, grand, valuable, cool and metallic.

Bronze: Warm, traditional, durable and rustic.

These are Silver Age Marvel Comics from the author's collection.

Derived from the ancient Greek word komikos and associated with comedy. Comics are a graphic-art medium that often involves the design of pictures and words arranged in sequence to convey an idea, information or a narrative. They can sometimes be wordless, instead utilising symbolism and conventions, such as word balloons, to represent speech.

☞ see Cartoon 57, Kirby, Jack 130, Speech Bubble 217

Thought-provoking and biting statements, combined with incisive drawing. Commentary has a long tradition in editorial illustration. Outlets for visual journalists include magazines, E-zines, animation, graphic novels and newspapers. Witty, satirical and humorous cartoons and caricatures are utilised to elucidate and amplify texts on political, cultural and social issues.

Illustration by Paul Bowman

☞ see Caricature 56, Editorial Illustration 87

AN INSTRUCTION OR ROLE GIVEN TO AN
ILLUSTRATOR BEFORE ACCEPTING A PROJECT.
COMMISSIONS COME FROM EDITORIAL AND
PUBLISHING FIELDS, DESIGN COMPANIES AND
ADVERTISING AGENCIES. IT IS IMPORTANT TO
AGREE ON THE FEE, USAGE RIGHTS AND TERMS
OF THE CONTRACT IN ADVANCE.

☞ see Advertising, 21

The ability to present and talk about one's work is fundamental in the illustration industry. Self awareness, interpersonal skills and confidence gained through listening and feedback are crucial for an illustrator.

'Things are cool' by Naja Conrad-Hansen

☛ see Commission 68, Pitch 177

The act of putting together, organising and arranging various elements in order to form a unified whole. This could apply to the creation of a work of art, music or written piece. The illustration above is called 'Messy Monster' – a bold and colourful composition by Rachel Ortas.

Images created by computers and specialist software in order to convey realism. CGI is used to animate scenes in feature films that would be too expensive or impossible to create normally. Realistic and complex motion can be simulated for a wide range of areas including entertainment, medical and scientific research, flight simulators or three-dimensional architectural virtual walk-throughs for the property market.

Cartwright Pickard Architects' winning entry for Living Steel shows strength of vision and visualisation. It allows both planners and the public to gain an insight into how a development will look.

A new form of illustration that looked beyond literal interpretation emerged during the 1950s and 1960s. Concept was key and illustrators incorporated puns, metaphors, wit, humour, symbolism and abstract and representational imagery into their visual commentaries. Illustrations embodied the complex dilemmas and concerns that affected this time of social and political upheaval and rapid technological change. The conceptual illustration below conveys the idea behind psychometric testing.

Illustration by Alex Robbins

☞ see **Push Pin Studios 191, Steinberg, Saul 220**

A legal device that protects the ownership of intellectual property. Governments grant exclusive rights to authors and creative artists to control the reproduction of their original works.

Pictorial matter created for commercial use such as company branding aimed at a specific target audience. This includes packaging, corporate websites, print advertisements, identities and logo design. Illustrators are also employed to create images for a company's Unique Selling Proposition (USP) or annual report.

This was one of five illustrations created for IBM's international
'What Makes You Special?' advertising campaign.

☞ see Advertising 21, Marketing 146

An acclaimed member of the Arts and Crafts Movement. His varied and prolific output included children's books, illustrations, paintings, political cartoons, ceramic tiles, stained glass, vases, mosaics, textile designs and wallpaper. An influential illustrator and designer, Crane established the Art Workers Guild. He was also director of design at the Manchester Municipal School and Principal of the Royal College of Art, London. Crane was influenced by the work of John Ruskin, the Pre-Raphaelite Brotherhood, the Renaissance, Japanese Ukiyo-e prints and socialism.

☞ see Arts and Crafts Movement 37, Children's Books 61

HEADS OF THE TABLE.

Caricaturist, social reformer and commentator often described as Britain's greatest book illustrator. The son of Scottish caricaturist Isaac Cruikshank, his prolific 70-year output included working in collaboration with Charles Dickens illustrating *Oliver Twist* (1838), and producing his own *Comic Almanac* (1835–1853) and illustrations, such as the one featured above. Working in the medium of wood and steel engraving, he chronicled both the social and political events of nineteenth-century London. Cruikshank was fiercely patriotic and also produced anti-French Napoleonic and anti-Irish rebellion propaganda.

☛ see Almanacs 24

A pivotal art movement initiated in 1907–1914 in Paris by Pablo Picasso (1881–1973) and Georges Braque (1882–1963). At the time, Picasso drew inspiration for Cubism from the simplicity and visual impact of primitive art, African masks, Iberian sculptures and the works of Paul Cézanne. Characteristics of analytic cubism include breaking, analysing and reforming objects, geometric space, removal of depth and depicting subjects from a range of viewpoints. Synthetic Cubism, the second phase of the movement, was important for the introduction of collage and *papier collé*, which used pasted newspaper cuttings, letter forms, wallpaper, wax, sheet music, paper cutouts, cloth and sand, amongst other items.

☞ see Assemblage 39, Collage 64

Life House Flexible's factory-made components mean this housing prototype (a shortlisted competition entry) can start in many different configurations, taking into account the occupants' evolving needs. This model was designed by Cartwright Pickard Architects.

Technical illustrations for instructional and maintenance manuals, journals, plans, encyclopedias and museum displays that use ghosted images to expose the internal workings of objects or machines. In the 1930s, illustrator Russell W Parker (1871–1949), nicknamed 'the cutaway man', pioneered the three-dimensional cutaway with pencil drawings of his military hardware designs and the inside details of telescopes. This technique was also explored in Japan by Yoshihiro Inomoto with his meticulous pen and ink automotive drawings.

☞ see Architectural Illustration 32

An international movement in the arts that was founded by Tristan Tzara in Zurich in 1916 and employed nihilism, ridicule and anti—art sentiment to negate the traditions, social conventions and moral values of capitalism. Dada was a forerunner of surrealism, pop art, the 1960s counter culture, situationism, postmodernism and punk.

☛ see Collage 64, Surrealism 227

One aspect of illustration is to create beautiful, ornamental images by adorning the page: this can be achieved through decoration. The use of decoration is evident throughout the history of the image from ancient rituals to religious artefacts and medieval illuminated manuscripts. Decoration is also found in wood-engraved chapter headings, tailpieces and vignettes for illustrated books.

This is the inside cover of a 1920s children's book.

☞ see Art Deco 34, Art Nouveau 36, Illuminated Manuscripts 121

Diagram by Mark Wigan

A symbolic drawing such as a graph, schematic sketch, plan or chart intended to clarify and explain how something works. It also shows interactions and relationships between parts and the whole. Illustrators use diagrams to aid idea generation, problem solving and to find new relationships between information. Different diagrams include flowcharts, maps, pie charts, radial and circuit diagrams, bubble maps, mind maps, matrices, tree and constellation diagrams, and graphs.

Charlotte Gould

Technological advances that have caused momentous
and radical changes to lifestyles around the world,
including the profession of illustration. The vast majority
of illustrators use computers as tools and they provide
great control, flexibility and power. Digital convergence
has enabled many aspects of the profession to be carried
out from the home or studio. The digital revolution is
providing new territories and opportunities for the
ancient art of illustration.

☞ see Computer-generated Imagery (CGI) 71

Innovative twentieth-century American entertainer, animator, producer, director, entrepreneur and philanthropist. Disney won 26 Oscars and seven Emmy Awards, the highest number ever awarded. Walt founded Walt Disney Productions with his brother Roy O. Disney. It is now a multi-billion dollar entertainment corporation. With animator Ub Iwerks, he created the most famous cartoon character in the world, Mickey Mouse.

An unfocused, aimless and informal drawing or scribble produced while preoccupied by something else or while killing time. The doodle can be seen as a speculative way of starting to solve a visual communication problem or as a means of intuitive visual experimentation.

☞ see Graffiti 108

French artist and illustrator who mainly worked with precise wood and steel engraving. His vast output of evocative literary illustration was noted for its supernatural landscapes, detail and use of light. Doré worked for a number of British publishers and produced work for the *Illustrated London News*. His book, *London: A Pilgrimage* (1872) featured 180 emphatic social reportage engravings exposing the slums and life of the poor in what was considered to be the capital of the world. The image below is Doré's 'Superintendent'.

The act of applying direct marks or lines across a surface
by using tools such as a pencil, pen and ink, charcoal or
crayons. Drawing is the foundation of all forms of visual
art and pictorial representation. Each artistic craft is a
method of drawing. Drawing is enquiry, observation,
speculation, consideration, critical reflection and
evaluation. It is both a creative and cognitive activity –
a key part of the illustrator's skill set.

This moving card was created by 3 Deep Design. The drawings convey
a collage-like and surreal feel.

☞ see Ideas 120

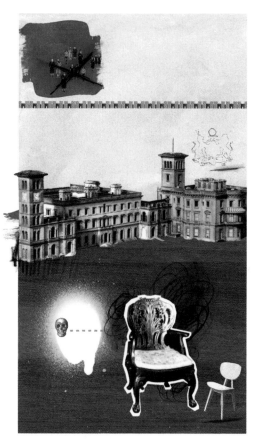

Editorial work commissioned by daily national and regional newspapers, weekend supplements, monthly lifestyle magazines, trade magazines, contract publishing and subscription titles. Editorial work involves responding to briefs for relatively low fees on tight deadlines. However, the regular space or column allows the illustrator to try new techniques and showcase work to a large audience.

This illustration was created by Caroline Tomlinson for *Transmission* magazine.
This was the illustrator's interpretation of a short story called 'When She was Queen'.

Illustrations that inform, clarify and help to provide knowledge, skills, instruction and wisdom. These types of images are usually found in children's books and magazines, and are designed to attract and engage with a young audience.

Tell Me Why, World of Wonder, and *Look and Learn* are magazines from the 1960s and 1970s that were published by IPC Magazines Ltd and Fleetway Publications Ltd.

A centuries-old art or handicraft that involves the decoration, ornamentation and embellishment of fabric or other material by the stitching of thread or yarn by hand or machine. The detailed needlework of embroidery can feature elaborate patterns, designs and illustrated sequential narratives.

☞ see Bayeux Tapestry 43, Knitted Illustration 132

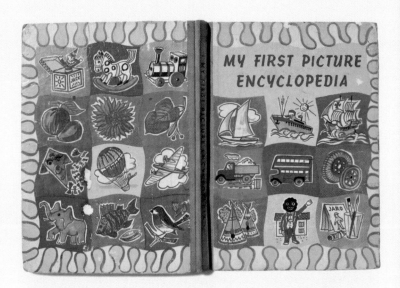

Derived from the Greek for a 'well-rounded education', encyclopedias are either general or subject specific. The earliest examples of these compendia to have survived were produced in Ancient Rome. Encyclopedias were later produced in medieval Europe, Islamic countries and China. Benchmarks include the 12 volumes of the French *Encyclopedie* (1762–1772), and the publication of the *Encyclopedia Britannica*. In the twenty-first century, Wikipedia has become a mainstream internet, user-generated content encyclopedias.

A great deal of illustration falls under the category of entertainment wherein its main function is to amuse and divert. Before digital video games and virtual worlds, illustrators provided charming and amusing images for board games such as Monopoly, Snakes and Ladders, Tiddley Skittles and Taxi.

Photography by Mark Wigan

This 1950s Taxi board game box is by Ariel.

☞ see Merchandising 150, Music Graphics 155

Images created to contribute to wayfinding projects and signage displayed in an outdoor environment. Illustration is commissioned to communicate brand identities for retail, entertainment and transport companies, and function as information design in the three-dimensional world. Environmental illustration can also encompass concept art for computer-game environments and collaborations with architects, landscape architects, graphic designers and industrial designers. Environmental art, along with land and installation art, often transforms natural and urban spaces with large-scale artworks, which provide a rich source of inspiration.

These are images from the Deptford Train Project in London designed by Studio Myerscough.

☞ see Information 125

A form of intaglio printmaking, the word derives from the Dutch word *etzen* meaning 'to eat'. An image is produced by a needle on a metal plate usually made of copper, zinc or steel, which has been coated with an acid-resisting ground. The plate is put into a mordant acid bath that etches the lines to the depth required. Faint lines can be protected by stop-out varnish. The darkness of the print is dependent on the depth of the line. After a series of bitings, the plate can be inked and wiped; the ink remains on the depressed lines or tones and is picked up on dampened paper by the etching press.

This etching, 'The Soldier and his Wife', was created by Daniel Kopfer – one of the first to apply the etching technique to print-making.

☞ see Printmaking 186

A code of conduct for individuals, groups or
organisations based on a set of principles and moral
values, which is increasingly incorporated into areas
such as illustration.

Illustration is a useful medium for conveying ethical and serious messages,
as seen below in the examples for Christian Aid. This project was designed by NB Studio.

Illustrations by NB Studio

☞ see Political Illustration 179

The act of trying out new things, ideas or techniques.
Pablo Picasso stated that art is 'a leap into the dark',
and in order to keep work vibrant, illustrators must
constantly experiment and visually mix materials, media
processes and methodologies.

This experimental abstract image was created by Kate Gibb for the
Chemical Brothers' 'Surrender' album art.

☞ see Avant-garde 41, Brainstorming 51

An art movement pioneered in Europe in the late nineteenth and early twentieth centuries, which emphasised the subjective and emotional inner expression of the artist over objective reality and traditional, formal compositions. Strong emotions were conveyed through distortion and the bold and symbolic use of colour.

This expressive 'Green Goddess' illustration is by UK-based Indian illustrator Janine Shroff, who graduated from Camberwell BA Illustration and Central St Martins MA Communication Design. Her idiosyncratic bird people images have been published in *Le Gun, DNA* newspaper and *The Guardian*.

A genre of illustration featuring fictional worlds and references to magical heroes, imaginary creatures, myths, legends, lost worlds, sorcery and the Middle Ages. The fantasy works of writers such as Lewis Carroll, J R R Tolkien, C S Lewis, Edgar Rice Burroughs, Rudyard Kipling and Robert E Howard have led to inspired interpretations by illustrators.

This fantasy illustration by Dan Seagrave combines decorative elements with ominous overtones and was used as an album cover for Demon Hunter on Solid State Records.

Drawings commissioned by designers required to visually communicate styles of apparel, accessories, cosmetics and hairstyles in the current mode.

This *Flaunt* magazine cover illustration was designed by Mario Hugo using graphite and china ink on acetone stained paper.

Illustration by Mark Wigan

An instrument used for drawing or writing with ink that flows from a tip made from pressed fibres. 'Magic Marker' is a trademarked name for a felt-tip pen.

☞ see Pen and Ink 167

The French phrase for 'end of the century'.
The term is associated with the Symbolists and the
Aesthetic movement, Art Nouveau, La Belle Epoque,
decadence and the anticipation of cultural upheaval
during the period between 1880 and 1914. It
characterised a historical period that was a
precursor of Modernism.

This illustration is by Aubrey Beardsley – a renowned British illustrator associated with the Aesthetic movement. He is renowned for his dark, sinuous and erotic images for Oscar Wilde's play *Salome* and contributions to *The Yellow Book*, *Savoy* and *Studio*.

www.CartoonStock.com

☞ see Art Nouveau 36, Beardsley, Aubrey 44, Symbolism 228

Direct marketing materials used to advertise an event.
In London during the early 1980s, photocopied designs
on different-coloured paper stock were used as a cheap
way to promote club events – they also became a way for
emerging illustrators to gain exposure for their work.

☞ see Music Graphics 155

Established in Britain in 1947 by Charles Ede, the Folio
Society aims to produce editions of the world's great
literature in a format worthy of the contents. The Folio
Society has published over 1,000 editions and has made
an important contribution to the illustrated book.
The works of Chaucer, Shakespeare and Dickens have
been interpreted by leading illustrators of their day, such
as Edward Bawden, Charles Keeping, Val Biro and
Simon Brett.

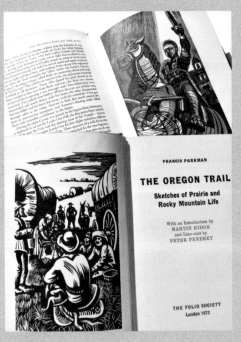

☛ see Narrative 156

A broad-ranging term originally used to describe the decorative arts and crafts of European peasants. It is also applied to objects made in America during the colonial period. Folk art has often inspired the work of artists such as Kandinsky. Many contemporary illustrators draw inspiration from this source.

☞ see Outsider Art 163

The French word for 'rubbing' that describes a technique first developed by surrealist artist Max Ernst in 1925. Ernst created a series of experimental drawings from rubbings taken from the patterns in the grain of old wooden floors, which he published as *Histoire Naturelle* in 1926. He utilised the technique on various textured surfaces and made use of it in what he termed 'grattage' – creating textures by scraping paint over objects. The image below is Max Ernst's *Fish-Bone Flowers*, 1928.

☞ see Surrealism 227

Categories that each have their own conventions and codes raising questions of narrativity, subjectivity and authorship. Popular genres and sub genres include fairytales, fables, westerns, comedy, adventure, biography, historical romance, horror, mystery, science fiction, fantasy, crime fiction, thrillers.

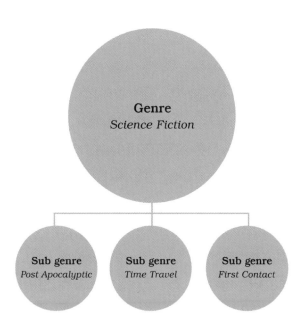

Genre
Science Fiction

Sub genre
Post Apocalyptic

Sub genre
Time Travel

Sub genre
First Contact

☞ see Narrative 156

Arguably the greatest political and social graphic satirist of all time. Gillray was a leading figure in the history of British illustration. With biting wit, he produced over 1,000 etchings ridiculing the vanity and social customs of his time. Gillray's prints were popular for their audacity, humour and delicate technique.

MATRIMONIAL-HARMONICS.

☞ see Humour 118, Satire 202

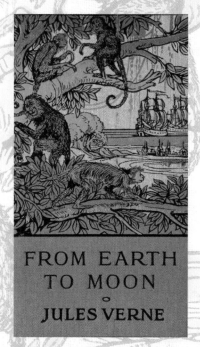

THE PERIOD BETWEEN THE 1880s AND THE 1920s,
WITNESSED A RISE IN THE QUALITY AND EXCELLENCE
IN PRINTED BOOK, MAGAZINE AND JOURNAL
ILLUSTRATION, FUELLED BY PUBLIC DEMAND AND
IMPROVEMENTS IN PRINTING TECHNOLOGY.
ILLUSTRATORS DREW INSPIRATION FROM THE PRE-
RAPHAELITE BROTHERHOOD, THE ARTS AND CRAFT
MOVEMENT, CELTIC ORNAMENT, JAPANESE COLOUR
PRINTS AND ART NOUVEAU.

☞ see Arts and Crafts Movement 37, Art Nouveau 36

An example of urban graffiti in Manhattan, New York, March 2008.

This term is derived from the Italian word *graffito* meaning 'scratched'. Graffiti ranges from carvings and scrawlings on property to aerosol spray painting of subway cars, vans and streets. Evidence of graffiti has been found in the ancient civilisations of the Mayans, Greeks and Romans, and it has always been associated with the conveyance of political, satirical or radical social messages.

This piece was designed by British graphic designer and illustrator Si Scott. He hand-draws his images with fine-liner pens and then scans and reduces them. The results demonstrate his love of integrating typography, drawing and design.

This term was first coined by designer William Addison Dwiggins in 1922. Graphic design is a profession, and an applied and practical visual art form. It is also a process of visualising and communicating concepts, ideas and messages through the effective combination of text and image. Graphic design integrates a range of skills and techniques such as typography, layout design and illustration. It can be applied in any media including motion graphics, animation, web design, packaging, signage, advertisements, posters, logos, magazines and books.

A term employed to market comic books with a lengthy unified narrative. Antecedents include the 1920s wordless woodcut novels of Frans Masereel and the Tintin albums of Hergé. The term 'graphic novel' became associated with Will Eisner and his *A Contract with God and Other Tenement Stories* in 1978.

British illustrator who, with Walter Crane, Randolph Caldecott and the colour printing of Edmund Evans, pioneered nineteenth-century children's book illustration. Although working at a time of mass production and urban squalor during the Industrial Revolution in Britain, Greenaway created an idyllic world in sentimental picture books with her beautifully crafted watercolour illustrations.

This illustration ('Polly'), by Kate Greenaway was taken from *The Queen of the Pirate Isle* by Bret Harte.

☞ see Alphabet Books 25, Crane, Walter 75, Golden Age 107

A folded card often featuring illustration or photography bearing a message for a specific occasion. Greetings cards are often sent on holidays and occasions to be remembered. Hand-made greetings cards were first sent by the Ancient Egyptians and the first commercially printed greetings card was the Christmas card, which was invented by Sir Henry Cole in 1846. Millions of printed cards are sold every year and virtual cards can also be sent by e-mail.

Happy Christmas

ho ho ho

and a happy new year

☞ see Merchandising 150

Illustration by James Brown

The act of drawing characters or symbols representing
speech. It is a personal and unique process that offers
limitless possibilities, expressiveness and spontaneity for the
illustrator. Hand lettering includes sign writing, contemporary
graffiti writing, inscriptions, embroidery and calligraphy. It
makes use of the skilful art of writing as opposed to the
systematic setting of type.

This example by James Brown was created for an article in
Sainsbury's magazine called 'How to Argue'.

☞ see Graphic Design 109, Typography 244

Illustrated botanical books dating back to the fifteenth
century. These books contained detailed illustrations
and descriptions of the magical and medicinal properties
of herbs and plants.

Shown here is an image from
Herbarium Blackwellianum, Volume IV.

Melo.

1. Blume
2. Frucht
3. Saame

Melonen
Pfeben.

☞ see Botanical Illustration 50

Sacred carvings and an ancient picture-writing system created by the Egyptians in which pictorial symbols represent sound, concepts and objects or a combination of these. They are phonetic and pictographic signs integrated with abstract and observational drawings. Colour was also used symbolically. The earliest illustrations to have survived are evident in papyrus rolls such as the *Book of the Dead* and the *Ramesseum Papyrus*.

☞ see Hand-drawn Type 113

Illustrations that depict past human activity and significant events in historically accurate settings. The internet has encouraged illustrators to explore historical imagery and find inspiration in visual languages from a vast range of eclectic sources.

☞ see Encyclopedia 90

British painter, cartoonist, printmaker, satirist, social commentator and philanthropist. Originally trained as a silversmith, Hogarth studied painting under Sir John Thornhill and produced sequential paintings and engravings. His engravings are now seen as precursors of the comic strip or graphic novel. In 1735, Hogarth successfully lobbied parliament to introduce the Engravers' Copyright Act. The illustration below is Hogarth's 'The Lecture'.

THE LECTURE.

"Yes, Gert, the Ministry can direct you to Charing Cross Road, or even Elephant and Castle."

"Another of those confounded quacks."

Photography by Mark Wilson

An element in illustration that can evoke laughter, happiness and feelings of amusement. Humorous illustrations can be found in gag cartoons, comics, caricatures and satirical cartoons, which employ parody, incongruity, metaphors, surprise, hyperbole and absurdity. The art of making people laugh has always been fundamental to illustration, comic books and cartooning and has made an important contribution to our artistic heritage.

☞ see Caricature 56, Cartoon 57

The tradition of using highly detailed pictorial representation. It is rooted in the sharp-focused naturalism and realist painting of the Dutch School of painters and the Pre-Raphaelites. Some illustrators specialising in hyperrealism produce intricate renderings conveying information for a wide range of contexts. Techniques and materials have ranged from detailed watercolours and oils to airbrushes and the latest digital software and hardware.

Portrait; oil on board by David Fulford

☛ see Rockwell, Norman 200

This work used a mixed-media technique and was created for an indoor campaign for a vintage clothes shop (art and design by José Palma at La Oveja Negra).

A thought or mental image formulated by consciousness, giving rise to concepts and knowledge. Illustrators solve specific problems for distinct audiences, while elucidating words pictorially through the generation of ideas and concepts. When first presented with a brief, illustrators generate ideas.

☞ see Brainstorming 51, Rockwell, Norman 200

Vellum or parchment
manuscripts dating
back to AD400.

They were developed in
monasteries and they are
adorned and decorated by
complex interlacing patterns,
initials, borders and miniature
illustrations painted in bright
tempera colours, as well as gold and silver leaf.

They were mainly produced for religious purposes
such as illuminated Christian Bibles and Islamic
manuscripts.

Influential British magazine established in 1998 combining fiction and poetry with work by emerging and established illustrators. Special issues have also acted as showcases for illustration students.

☛ see Magazines 143

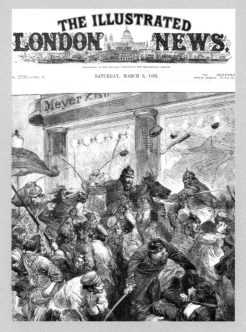

Founded by Herbert Ingram and Mark Lemon in 1842, *The Illustrated London News* was published weekly until 1971 and monthly and quarterly in later years. The influential publication was large format and contained 16 pages with 30 engravings per issue. Victorian illustrators drew eyewitness images that were sent as quickly as possible to woodblock engravers for reproduction. These pictorial journalists brought news from all over the British Empire, covering expeditions, disasters, art exhibitions, political events, Paris fashions, wars and new inventions during the Industrial Revolution.

The ability to form new ideas, concepts and images. This creative and resourceful faculty is essential for visualisation and problem solving. Imagination is vital for illustrators in order to create work that is meaningful, innovative, unusual and original. The image below shows that imagination produces unique interpretations, which combine logical thinking with intuition.

Illustration by Andy Potts

☞ see Brainstorming 51

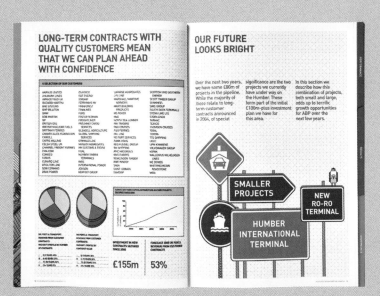

Illustration by Johnny Kelly

A broad and diverse field of illustration that documents, instructs and explains through a wide variety of visual languages. Outlets include instructional diagrams, maps, pictographs, encyclopedias, educational textbooks, interactive design and web interface design.

This annual report by NB Studio delivers information with clarity and a clean, contemporary tone.
A series of colourful and detailed illustrations suggest the scale and complexity of the client's business.

see Diagram 81

n brilliant or timely idea. Creative inspir
n breaking away from routine, going fo
visiting a cinema, a library, a flea mark
travelling to another country. Building a
g a digital camera and notebook hand
establish links between inspiring ideas a

A global network that connects millions of computers, in order to share and exchange information from small and large networks. The internet has completely changed the visual communication industry. Illustrators are now able to network, seek new business opportunities and deliver their work to clients globally via the internet.

☞ see Websites 260

Illustration by Tom Barwick

The intellectual analysis and process of translating and explaining. Illustrators employ interpretation to elucidate, illuminate and amplify written language with their own use of visual language. The ability to create a world and explain a narrative, an idea or theme pictorially is the fundamental activity of illustration. Interpreting text must take into consideration plot development, mood, rhythm and pace of the narrative.

This illustration is one of a series interpreting specific texts for Tom Barwick's publication, *Ratio*.

The conscious act of arranging or placing visual
elements side by side to show similarities and
differences. Illustrators utilise witty juxtapositions
combined with other visual devices, such as similes
or metaphors. By positioning contrasting images next
to one another, a series of meanings and associations
can be produced. The use of surprising contrasts runs
throughout the work of many humorous illustrators
such as W Heath Robinson and his compilations
of drawings in *Absurdities* (1934).

Connections or contrasts are highlighted and implied when two
images are placed side by side.

Nicknamed 'King', Jack Kirby was a hugely influential and prolific American comic book artist and writer. His dynamic portrayals of urban combat were inspired by gang fights on New York's Lower East Side's tenement rooftops in the 1930s. He is responsible for co-creating legendary super heroes at Marvel Comics such as The Hulk, The Fantastic Four, X Men and Captain America. Kirby revolutionised comics by drawing thousands of pages with dynamic cinematic techniques, distortions, exaggerated perspectives, crackling dots of energy, centre spreads and photomontage.

This is an image taken from the author's Silver Age Marvel Comics collection.

☞ see Comics 66

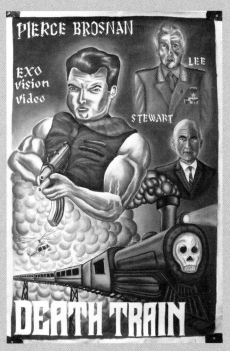

Death Train painting by Camberwell illustration graduate, Will Rigby.

The German word associated with trash, cheapness, vulgarity, pretentious art and popular, sentimental, commercial culture. The so-called kitsch commercial art of comics, pulp fiction, advertisements and magazine covers was viewed as the opposite to high art – an inferior art. However, the appropriation of kitsch has been a recurring theme in modern art from Dada and Surrealism to Pop Art and Postmodernism.

☞ see Dada 79, Surrealism 227

The act of creating illustration and images by using pointed needles and yarn to create a series of interlocking loops. Due to the popularity of the DIY, handicraft renaissance and Debbie Stoller's book, *Stitch 'n' Bitch*, knitting clubs have spread throughout the world and knitted illustrations appear in galleries and magazines. Knitted items are now considered fashion accessories.

These designs by Studio Myerscough show a contemporary approach to typographic design through the use of knitting.

☞ see Embroidery 89

DIE ÜBERLEBENDEN   **KRIEG DEM KRIEGE!**

THE SOCIALIST GERMAN ARTIST HIGHLY REGARDED FOR HER EXPRESSIVE GRAPHIC DEPICTIONS OF THOSE AFFECTED BY POVERTY, STARVATION AND WAR. SHE CREATED A POWERFUL BODY OF WORK, WHICH GRADUALLY DEVELOPED FROM NATURALISM INTO GERMAN EXPRESSIONISM. HER OUTPUT INCLUDED WOODCUTS, LITHOGRAPHY, ETCHING, DRAWING AND SCULPTURE.

☞ see Expressionism 96

A SERIES OF ANTHOLOGY-STYLE BOOKS EDITED BY SAMMY HARKHAM. IT HAS EVOLVED FROM A ZINE INTO AN OVER-SIZED, FULL-COLOUR BOOK OF CUTTING-EDGE GRAPHIC NARRATIVE.

☞ see Blab! 46, Zines 271

Le Gun is packed with strange and oblique narratives and intricate and beguiling black-and-white drawings. It was established at the Royal College of Arts in London in 2004 by Communication Art and Design students Bill Bragg, Alex Wright, Neal Fox, Matthew Appleton, Chris Bianchi and Rob Green.

☛ see Magazines 143

Drawing the human figure based on a live model, who
is usually nude. It is a fundamental activity for a student
of illustration. This activity involves the co-ordination
of the eye, brain and hand. It improves on skills such
as comparing relationships and proportions, framing,
assessing negative and positive space, and being aware
of internal structure and the three-dimensional
volume of a figure.

☞ see Observational Drawing 160

A mark created by the trace of a point in motion. There are few straight lines present in nature. A contour line is an illusion applied in drawing, which encloses form and creates a boundary. Lines have many properties that can communicate emotions and ideas. They can be rhythmic, strong, energetic, agitated, graceful, controlling, subtle and vigorous.

A relief printmaking method developed as an easier
alternative to producing woodcuts. As linoleum has no
grain, it can be cut in any direction. Linocuts are created
by carving and cutting into linoleum with knives or
gouges. The surface uncut areas are inked and printed,
producing a reversed mirror image.

☞ see Drawing 86, Printmaking 186

Invented by Alois Senefelder in 1797, it is a planographic process based on the antipathy of water and grease – the image repels water but accepts ink. Images are drawn on to a surface in litho crayon or oily ink; the flat surface is then treated with gum arabic and the ink is washed off, while the stone retains the grease. Prints are made from zinc, aluminium plate or stone with subtle graduations of tone and texture. Colour lithography or chromolithography was developed in 1837 by using separate stones and drawings for each colour used.

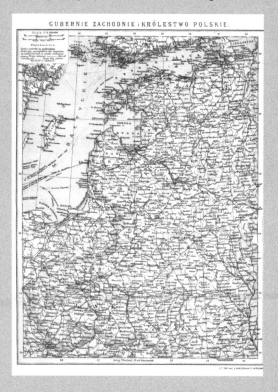

The act of painting in front of a live audience, usually associated with mural painting, graffiti and street art. Live painting performances emerged out of New York's East Village art scene and club culture in the 1980s. Key influences from New York include Jean-Michel Basquiat and Keith Haring. The images below show a live-painting event in Hitachinaka, Japan.

Photograph of live-painting event in Hitachinaka, Japan, by Mark Wigan

☛ see Paint 165

This image is from an illuminated manuscript of the *Rubaiyat of Omar Khayam*. The calligraphy and ornamentation were done by William Morris.

handwritten marginal note: one might say the same of Building Stories (Chris Ware) & WaterLife (2012) but these are ebook reactionaries.

Expensive and lavishly made with high-quality materials, these artists' books were usually made in a small edition and associated with the French bibliophile tradition and private presses. The books were produced for collectors as a reaction to the poor quality of products being commercially printed during the Industrial Revolution. William Morris is a key figure in the tradition, making his own handmade books and forming the Kelmscott Press in 1891.

☞ see Book Art 48, Folio Society 102

Studio Output's design for The Coca-Cola Company uses illustration that effectively conveys the product and harmonises with the brand and logo.

A recognisable emblem, symbol, sign or icon designed with letterforms or logotype to form a trademark that denotes a specific institution, company or brand. Graphical logo designs are used to embody brands and provide instant recognition. Ideograms (signs, icons, emblems or symbols) are employed with logotypes to communicate across cultures and languages. Iconic logos include the Red Cross, Nike's 'swoosh', the Playboy Bunny and the Coca-Cola logo.

☞ see Corporate Illustration 74, Marketing 146

A periodic publication aimed at the general public, often published weekly or monthly. It contains articles, advertisements, illustrations and photographs. The word magazine derives from the Arabic word *makahazin*, which means 'warehouse'.

Constructivism, Art Deco and Modernism informed the design of magazines such as *Vogue*, *Fortune* and *Vanity Fair* in twentieth-century America. Outstanding illustrators such as Norman Rockwell, J C Leyendecker, Al Parker, Robert Weaver and Saul Steinberg visually communicated the aspirations and concerns of millions through the medium of the printed magazine.

This is the cover for *Journal des Voyages* – a magazine popular in the 1890s.

☛ see Rockwell, Norman 200, Steinberg, Saul 220

The Japanese word for humorous pictures,
printed cartoons, comics and graphic
novels recognisable for stylised
conventions such as large and round
eyes. Popular manga published in Japan are
sometimes adapted into animé – Japanese
animation. Subject matter ranges from the
humorous, romantic and violent to the
sexually explicit.

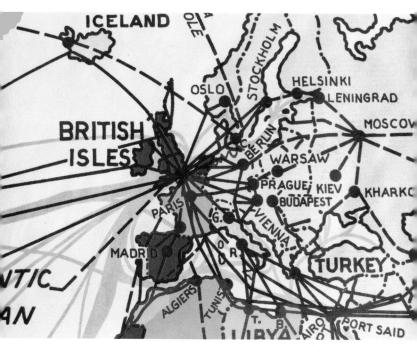

Throughout the development of civilisation, mapping the known world has been an essential activity. Cartography and topography were created for military campaigns, voyages of conquest, exploration, pilgrimages, trade routes and scientific surveys. Maps for leisure were also produced. In the 1920s and 1930s, Ordnance Survey maps of the British Isles became hugely popular for motoring, cycling and walking tours.

☛ see Information 125

Illustrations are used in marketing and advertising to create images that promote brands and communicate company values. Marketing manages, identifies and anticipates customers' needs and relationships to products. The art of illustration can be employed as part of a campaign to create desire, catch the eye or stimulate action to launch new products and services, or rebrand established ones.

This book cover design was for a travelogue based on the author's experiences in and around Colombia and its drug trade.

Illustration by Andy Potts

Illustration by Anthony Fournier

The act of making and arranging traces or marks, such as lines, with a tool. Mark making can increase confidence and mastery of tools and materials, as well as extend the illustrator's visual vocabulary. Experimenting and using as many methods as possible helps build the illustrator's unique personal visual language.

☞ see Drawing 86

An important graphic artist and painter, Masereel produced more than 20 wordless, woodcut graphic novels. Full of social and political comment and incisive direct observation, his work would in time come to influence the development of the comic book and the graphic novel. Pictured above is Masereel's *Hotel*, 1925.

☞ see Graphic Novels 110

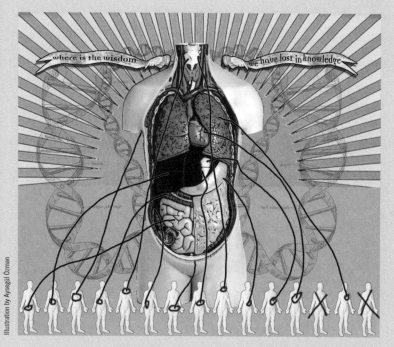

Early medical illustrations in medieval manuscripts were informed by classical scholarship and not observation. This changed with the publication of Andreas Vesalius's groundbreaking anatomical woodcuts, *Epitome De Humani Corporis Fabrica* in 1542. Contemporary medical illustration is a diverse field encompassing instructional, informative, educational and clinical material. Today, medical illustrations include traditional anatomical images, surgical operations, patient health care information, scientific diagrams, posters, textbooks, encyclopedias and TV documentaries. Various media are utilised to elucidate information such as 3D models, animations, painting and digital imaging.

An important income generator for illustrators whose characters created for books and/or animated films can be made into a vast range of products. Artwork can be produced for promotional tie–ins such as novelty goods, cards, games, toys, textiles, clothing and figurines. Illustrators retain the copyright of the artwork and grant licences for specific use on products over a certain time period and for certain territories. The illustrator is usually involved in quality control and ensures that the merchandise is satisfactory.

☞ see Greetings Cards 112, T-shirt 243

Illustrations that combine elements from a number of different media, such as paints, inks, pastels, pencils and the introduction of found objects and ephemera. Contemporary illustrators often utilise scanners and digital cameras, mixing hand-crafted elements with digital effects.

Poster design for Montreal's La Ronde theme park promoting their 'La Nuit Blanche' event.

Illustration by Andy Potts

☞ see Experimentation 95

A unique print often created by placing paper on artwork that is produced on a metal plate or glass, and then printing via an etching or litho press. Variations are created depending on how the plate is inked. Mono prints can be created in many ways including collage, hand-colouring, working directly on to a screen and forcing the ink through with a squeegely. The image below is a mono print by Ceri Amphlett.

Decorative images constructed from small cubes of
coloured stone, ceramic, glass or marble. Mosaics were
used extensively by the Romans for floor and wall
decorations. Religious themes are portrayed in
outstanding examples by Byzantine artists of mosaic in
Constantinople (now Istanbul). The image above is of
a mosaic by Jane Sybilla Fordham.

☞ see Vienna Secession 252

Paintings on large walls, ceilings and buildings that visually communicate ideas and messages to large audiences and specific communities. Murals have existed for centuries and can be found in prehistoric cave paintings; the walls of ancient Egyptian tombs; Greek and Roman frescos; churches of the Middle Ages; and seventeenth-century European palaces. Murals range from the decorative tradition of trompe l'oeil (trick of the eye) to the propaganda murals of totalitarianism. Murals are art for the people – they function outside of the established gallery-based art world. Influential muralists include Michelangelo, Raphael, Diego Rivera, Judy Baca, Keith Haring and the Bogside Artists.

Murals in the Lower East Side of Manhattan, New York, March 2008.

This album cover was designed and illustrated by Johnny Kelly at NB Studio. The cover was designed for Birdman Ray; old woodcuts were used with a contemporary twist.

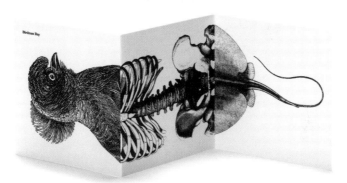

Artwork commissioned by the music industry to promote and identify a musician or band's work. An innovative field of expression for illustrators and designers, iconic examples have defined and reflected the development of popular and visual culture. Music graphics attract potential purchasers and communicate the values associated with the product. Constantly evolving and adapting, the field has developed from iconic vinyl record sleeves to CDs to providing visual content for downloads, websites, branding, videos, set design and merchandise.

☞ see Campaign 55, Marketing 146

This was a piece created for *Beast* internet magazine in answer to a brief called 'Imitation'.

From the word *narrare*, which means 'to recount', a narrative is the telling of a story or an account of events in a coherent sequence. Events, characters and settings are arranged in a consistent and meaningful framework by the illustrator in order to convey the storyline visually. Maurice Sendak stated that his intention as an illustrator was to let the story speak for itself with his pictures acting as a kind of background music – music in the right style, always in tune with the words.

The interpretation of fictional or non-fictional events through pictorial storytelling is at the heart of the ancient art of illustration. Illustrators use their art to charm, entertain, educate and engage the imagination.

☞ see Cruikshank, George 76

The sciences related to the rational study and laws of the physical world and its phenomena, which employ illustrators to draw in areas such as botany, biology, chemistry, astronomy, zoology and physics.

'Fauna Amazonia' copyright Alan Male

☞ see Botanical Illustration 50, Herbals 114

THE
NEW YORKER

Founded in 1925 by Harold Ross, who set out to publish a magazine that would be distinguished by its illustrators. The cartoonists of the *New Yorker* are noted for reflecting and defining the times with disarming humour and sophisticated wit. The *New Yorker's* humour came in the form of single panel cartoons wryly directed at the middle-class American audience. Peter Arno, Charles Addams, Saul Steinberg, Mary Petty and William Steig are notable contributors to the publication.

☛ see Humour 118, Magazines 143

A portable pad of paper that can be used for jotting down ideas, observations and quick sketches, which may inform current or future projects. Ideas can come at any time, so it is important to get them down on paper before they are forgotten.

Illustration requires attentiveness and sustained practice and notebooks exist to be filled. The immediacy of a notebook sketch can sometimes provide a direct answer to a brief and can be scanned into the computer. Notebooks are also a way of reflecting on progress.

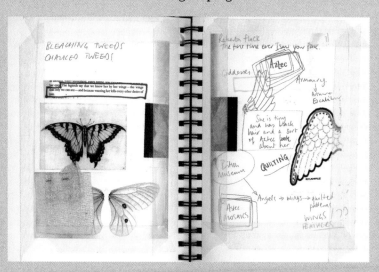

The above notebook by Becky French demonstrates how eclectic and varied a resource a notebook can become. It can act as a collection of 'found' items and as a working tool, helping an illustrator work through a series of ideas.

☞ see Sketchbook 215

Illustration by Chris Dent

The act of watching the world and recording three-dimensional objects on to a flat surface with an instrument. Through looking, scrutiny, awareness and hand-eye-brain co-ordination, lines, shapes, edges and space relationships are generated and manipulated by the illustrator.

Observational drawing is seen as an essential building block in the education of an illustrator. In his 1896 manual for students, *The Illustration of Books*, Joseph Pennell stated: 'You must draw, draw, draw first, last and all the time and until you can draw and draw well, you cannot illustrate.'

☞ see Life Drawing 136, Notebook 159

There are many groups that support and promote the interests of illustrators. Most of these groups have annuals that promote illustrators' works.

Some international organisations for illustrators:

The Association of Illustrators (UK)

The Society of Artists' Agents (UK)

The Graphic Artists' Guild

The Society of Publication Designers

The Society of Children's Book Writers and Illustrators

Guild of Natural Science Illustration

Association of Medical Illustration (USA)

Le Maison des Artistes (France)

Tokyo Illustrators' Society

☞ see Self Promotion 208

Ornithology is the scientific study of birds. During the eighteenth century, illustrators set out to survey and classify all forms of nature around the world. The growth of the British Empire and the Industrial Revolution of the nineteenth century made London the leading city for the publication of lithographic volumes and imperial folios on birds from around the world including those of Edward Lear and John Gould. A pioneer in the field was American naturalist John James Audubon, who created hand-coloured metal engravings for the outstanding four-volume, double-elephant folio, *The Birds of America* (1827-1838).

'Birds of Paradise' by Jake Blanchard

Illustration by Daniel Brereton

Visionary Museum, Baltimore, MD

Drawings, paintings and constructions created by untrained artists; it is also related to the works produced by psychiatric patients, prisoners or artists with strong cultural traditions. In 1945, Jean Dubuffet coined the term 'art brut' to describe artistic works that didn't imitate gallery art, but appealed to humanity's first origins. Key features include physiognomisation, *horror vacui*, meticulous line, absence of differentiation and use of mixed media.

The design of outer wrappings or encasements used to contain, protect and promote a product. Illustration is often employed to identify, label and help sell products via their packaging. Illustration plays an important role in packaging design, conveying a sense of what a product is, its values and characteristics.

Art direction by 3 Deep Design

The above images feature fragrances created by six renowned perfumers working with six celebrated designers. A percentage of the net proceeds will go towards awareness and funding for the charity Designers Against AIDS (DAA) and the International AIDS Awareness Education Center in Antwerp, Belgium.

☞ see Advertising 21, Graphic Design 109

Acrylic

Enamel

Gouache

Oil

Spray-paint

Watercolour

Ground pigments, thinners, binder and solvents in a liquid used to decorate, adorn or protect with thin coatings usually applied with a brush.

Types of paint

Acrylic: made from acrylic polymer emulsion; quick drying
Enamel: oil-based, glossy paint giving a smooth, hard coat
Gouache: opaque water paint with pigments suspended in water
Oil: has pigment particles suspended in oil; slow drying
Spray paint: air-compressed paint used to coat surfaces
Watercolour: made with water-soluble binders and thinned with water instead of oil

☞ see Acrylic 20, Watercolour 259

Vegetable fibres broken into cellulose pulp, drained through suspension in water and then dried and processed into rolls or sheets. This thin material is available in a range of weights, colours and textures and is widely used for drawing, writing and printing. Although it was first produced in China in the second century AD, paper was not used in Europe until the twelfth century. There is a huge range of papers of varying thicknesses and sizes available to the illustrator. Medium paper with a slight tooth can break up the lines of the drawing, giving it character. Bristol board, illustration boards, bond or graphic papers can be utilised for pen drawing. Heavier papers are used for watercolours. Paper that needs to be dampened is used for intaglio printing, and thin papers are generally used for relief printing.

General paper types:

Newsprint

Paper made primarily of mechanically ground newspapers, comics and wood pulp. It has a shorter lifespan than other papers, but it is cheap to produce.

Antique

A high-quality paper with a clay coating on both sides, which gives a good printing surface.

Uncoated woodfree

The largest printing and writing paper category. Most office paper and stationery is printed on this stock.

Tracing

A thin, translucent paper that allows light through, enabling artists to transfer images by tracing.

Art

Useful for halftones where definition and detail are important.

Cartridge

A thick white paper particularly used for pencil and ink drawings; adds texture to publications.

A drawing process or technique used by illustrators whereby an image is created by applying a coloured ink to a surface with a stylus or pen. Illustrators producing images for periodicals, newspapers and books were often referred to as black-and-white artists. Inks can be waterproof or non-waterproof and can be obtained in ink sticks or as liquid.

Types of pens include crow quills, cane and reed pens, dip and fountain pens with metal points, technical pens, mapping and lettering pens, fibre-tip pens, felt-tip pens and the ballpoint pen patented by László Biro in 1938.

Various pens convey individual styles and personalities, as seen in the examples below.

Quill

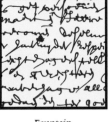
Fountain

Ballpoint

☞ see Felt-tip Pens 99, Pencil 168

9H 8H 7H 6H 5H 4H 3H 2H H F HB B 2B 3B 4B 5B 6B 7B 8B 9B

Hardest   Medium   Softest

The term 'pencil' referred to a pointed watercolour brush before the introduction of the lead pencil at the beginning of the nineteenth century. A versatile and expressive tool, it can be sharpened to a point for precise and eloquent mark-making. They range from wooden graphite pencils graded 8H (the hardest) to 8B (the softest), with HB being in the middle. Different types include clutch and propelling pencils, coloured pencils, charcoal, chalk and crayon pencils.

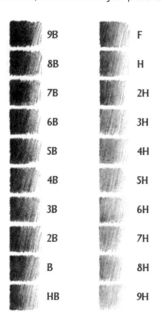

9B   F

8B   H

7B   2H

6B   3H

5B   4H

4B   5H

3B   6H

2B   7H

B   8H

HB   9H

☞ see **Mark Making 147**

Neon sculpture and illustration by Pure Evil for an exhibition at Ink-d gallery, Brighton, UK, 2008.

Self-initiated work enabling illustrators to experiment with new working methodologies and processes, which broaden techniques and skills. Experimental personal projects, such as self-published books, editions of prints, T-shirts and short films show clients the kind of work artists are passionate about and how their work could be applied to specific projects.

☞ see Commission 68, Client 62

A figure of speech utilised by illustrators to transfer human attributes to a concept or inanimate object. Examples include sports mascots, corporate promotional characters and national personifications, such as England's John Bull from the 1790s drawn by James Gillray, Thomas Rowlandson and George Cruikshank.

Illustration by Daniel Brereton

☞ see Anthropomorphism 30, Character 59

Illustration by Chris Dent

A scientific system developed by artists during the
Renaissance, which creates the illusion of three-dimensional
solid objects on the two-dimensional plane surface. Linear
perspective is based on parallel lines receding and converging
on the horizon line's vanishing point. Objects are drawn
smaller as they recede in space. One-, two- and three-point
perspective create the illusion of depth. Aerial perspective is
based on the idea that atmospheric conditions blur outlines
and affect the colour of objects at a distance.

Exaggerated perspective was employed for its psychological
effects in expressionist art, film noir and in the work of graphic
artists such as Frank Miller.

☞ see Architectural Illustration 32

A form of communication used to influence actions or beliefs by appealing to reason or emotions. Illustrators create symbolic images commissioned for propaganda, education, entertainment and advertising in order to win over their target audience. From Alfred Leete's famous wartime poster 'Your Country Needs You' (1914) to mobile phone billboards, illustration captures the public's imagination, targeting the emotions and desires of specific audiences in order to seduce, shock, educate, control, entertain and sell.

This piece by James Brown is a one-colour linocut illustrated in a manner that suits the copy – very polite and gentlemanly.

☞ see Advertising 21

The above are assorted zines created on a photocopier.

Photocopiers have been adopted by illustrators, artists and designers as a creative tool. In the 1970s, before the extensive use of computers, light-sensitive Xerox machines were used by illustrators to manipulate imagery and to publish artists' books, comics and fanzines. Digital laser copiers became key tools for illustrators in the late 1980s and early 1990s.

see Zines 271

Derived from the Greek word *photos* meaning 'light' and *graphos* meaning 'drawing'. Photography is the art of using a camera to capture an image on a light-sensitive plate via the chemical action of light. Many illustrators use photography to gather visual reference material, supplementing personal observations and drawings.

These images show photographs combined with print-making techniques. The images were created by Kate Gibb for *Jalouse* magazine.

☞ see Animation 28, Photomontage 175

Also described by contemporary digital illustrators and visualisers as compositing, photomontage is a technique that creates a new composite image by superimposing, combining or merging photographic images from different sources.

Dada, surrealist and constructivist artists such as John Heartfield, Salvador Dalí, Alexander Rodchenko and El Lissitzky pioneered the use of photomontage for shocking visual impact. The technique has also been adopted by commercial artists for the advertising industry from the early twentieth century onwards.

Illustration by Priya Sundaram

☞ see Collage 64, Photography 174

A visual symbol or reference used to communicate a word, letter, message, idea or phrase. Many written languages such as Chinese use pictogrammatic characters. Pictograms appear throughout the history of illustration and have been used extensively throughout the twentieth century to identify corporations, products and brands, and to instruct and inform.

Pictogram or Symbol
This pictogram is an image of a recognisable dog.

Ideogram
The ideogram is depicted by the red circle and line, which give the message: 'no'.

Icon
The bone is not an obvious image of a dog, but it represents and conveys the same message.

Logo
The logo is a graphic interpretation of a dog.

☞ see Rebus 193, Symbolism 228

To show or promote work to a potential client in order
to convince them to buy your work or services. Face-to-
face pitches are now rare as many illustration jobs are
commissioned via agents or by clients selecting
illustrators through work seen in annuals or on-line
portfolios. Thorough research about a potential client
is key to a successful pitch.

The Oxfam advertisement above uses immediate and rhetorical
illustrative text for visual impact.

☞ see Advertising 21

The Polish School of Poster Art emerged in the late 1950s and produced some of the most compelling images in graphic art. By 1966, the International Poster Biennial was held in Poland and in 1968, the world's first poster museum was established in Warsaw. The intelligent, poetic, bold and surreal posters designed for cultural events were seen as an art form of equal importance to paintings in galleries.

☛ see Conceptual Illustration 72, Poster, The 184

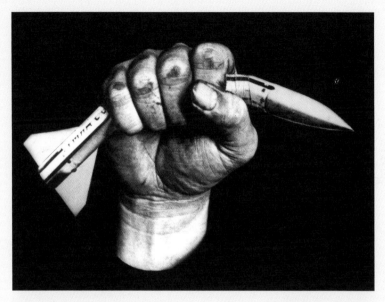

Illustration associated with protest, propaganda, satire and comment. Some iconic political graphic images include Latin graffiti in Pompeii, the biting satire of English caricaturists, Goya's 'The Disasters of War', the work of George Grosz, Alfred Leete's 'Your Country Needs You' war poster, Cuban revolutionary posters and posters for Amnesty International and CND.

This powerful photomontage is Crushed Missile (1980) by Peter Kennard. Kennard's prolific output included numerous posters and banners for the Campaign for Nuclear Disarmament (CND) in the 1980s.

A book that creates a three-dimensional structure that rises when a page is turned. Illustrated pop-up books often feature cut-outs and tabs that are pulled to move and enhance the meaning of the imagery. Pop-up books can function as freestanding sculptures and utilise a variety of inventive techniques such as flaps to open, fold-outs, pull-out tabs, rotating wheels and small books inserted in pockets.

Pop-up display by Mio Yoshi

A constantly updated portable selection of images arranged sequentially to showcase an illustrator's work and capture a prospective client's attention. Orchestrating the narrative flow of the portfolio and selecting the right illustrations for the specific client is an important process. Portfolios can come in various sizes and can range from standard zip-up portfolios to expensive high-quality leather-bound folios with clear sleeves. Many illustrators now display their work via online portfolios.

see Self Promotion 208, Websites 260

This dramatic portrait in oils (*Untitled*) was exhibited at the BP Portrait Award Exhibition by Camberwell BA Hons Illustration and RCA MA Communication graduate David Fulford.

An artistic representation of a person that can promote, flatter, analyse or make a comment. Portraits could represent a person's emotions, personality, status, identity or psyche.

In the 1891 novel *The Picture of Dorian Gray*, Oscar Wilde wrote: 'Every portrait painted with feeling is a portrait of the artist, not the sitter.' Portraits that involve the artist's interpretation and point of view include Rembrandt's self portraits at different stages of his life, Picasso's cubist portraits and Leonardo da Vinci's *Mona Lisa*.

☞ see Observational Drawing 160, Paint 165

Small rectangular cards used to send a message by post without the need of an envelope. One side of the card is written on and the other side often features an illustration or photograph, which can function as souvenirs. Since the nineteenth century, the simple rectangular piece of card has provided illustrators with a distinctive platform for their artwork. Highly collectable, picture postcards have documented and reflected the social history of their times. Humour is a popular theme and the prolific illustrator Donald McGill is renowned for his popular and saucy seaside postcards.

A small, illustrated, monthly chronicle published in London, which reflects the popular interest in collecting posters. It features poster designs from around the world including ones by M Yendis, John Hassall, Alphonse Mucha and the Beggarstaff Brothers.

☞ see Polish Posters 178

An English author and illustrator whose work has been adored by children for generations. The famous characters she invented in her books include Peter Rabbit, Squirrel Nutkin, Benjamin Bunny and Mrs Tiggy Winkle. Potter was an outstanding storyteller and watercolourist. She is also highly regarded as a scientific observer, landscapist and recorder of the natural world. In her sketchbook journals, she combined writing with precise renderings from nature including skilful paintings of fossils and fungi, constantly experimenting in a variety of styles and techniques.

Relief printing
Ink is left 'sitting' on a raised surface.

Intaglio
Ink is forced into slots or grooves.

Lithography
A damp roller goes before the inking roller,
making ink stick only to dry areas.

Screenprinting
Ink is forced through a mesh, following the
stencil pattern.

A category of art or design involving the process of reproducing single or multiple images by transferring them from one surface to another. Images are usually reproduced on a flat, prepared surface such as a plate, block or screen, and printed using ink on paper. Printmaking is constantly developing and can incorporate the use of numerous media.

The main categories of printmaking:
Relief printing: making use of a raised printing surface (cutting or engraving wood or linoleum).
Intaglio methods: etching with the imagery depressed below the plate's surface.
Planographic: lithography printing on a flat surface and exploiting the antipathy
between water and grease.
Screenprinting: using ink through stencils.
Digital printmaking: using archival inks, inkjet and laser printers.

☞ see Lithography 139, Screen Printing 207

The distinctive visual language of the 1960s counterculture pioneered by the work of rock poster artists such as Wes Wilson, Victor Moscoso, Alton Kelley, Rick Griffin, and Haphash and Coloured Coat. The posters mirrored the spirit of their times and the postmodern appropriation of historical poster art.

A live, psychedelic, acid house installation in Nagoya, Japan, in 1988.

☞ see Art Nouveau 36

This term is derived from the pulp paper that magazines used to be printed on. Colourful cover art played a vital role in the advertising of cheap pulp fiction magazines between the 1920s and 1950s, as well as paperbacks published since the 1950s. Some of the pulp fiction cover illustrators such as Virgil Finlay, Edd Cartier and Frank R. Paul became highly popular and collectable for their sensational and exotic covers.

☞ see Book Jacket 49, Magazines 143

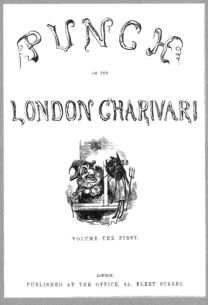

A popular British satirical humour magazine founded in 1841.
Punch was named after the puppet 'Mr Punch' or 'Punchinello'
and was published 1841–1992 and 1996–2002. Nineteenth-
century developments in printing, such as steel-plate
stereotyping and wood-engraved illustrations allowed text and
image to be integrated on *Punch*'s pages.

In 1843, *Punch* was credited with the first use of the word
'cartoon' to describe funny pictures. It provided exposure for
some of the greatest illustrators including Richard Doyle,
George Du Maurier, John Tenniel, Ronald Searle and
Gerald Scarfe.

An anarchic music, art and street
fashion subculture with a visual style
characterised by the illustrations,
collage techniques and graphics of artists
such as Bazooka, Barney Bubbles, Malcolm
Garrett, Neville Brody, Jamie Reid and
Peter Saville.

This Punk-Graphix, cut-and-paste illustration was produced for a fanzine.

☞ see Dada 79, Music Graphics 155

Founded in New York by Milton Glaser, Seymour Chwast, Reynold Ruffins and Edward Sorel in 1954. The studio responded to the minimal modernist international design style of the 1960s and had an illustrative, conceptual, inventive, humorous and eclectic approach. The founders incorporated diverse influences into their illustrations including Renaissance painting, Art Nouveau, Victorian type and comic books. The studio launched its own promotional journal: the influential and collectable *Push Pin Graphic*.

☞ see Conceptual Illustration 72, Magazines 143

Any image that is made from pixels, such as a photograph. A raster image can reproduce intricate tones. However, images are of fixed resolutions so they cannot be scaled, and image files tend to be large. Rasters come in two main types: CMYK (cyan, magenta, yellow, black) and RGB (red, green, blue). CMYK images contain more colours, or channels, and they are larger than RGB images.

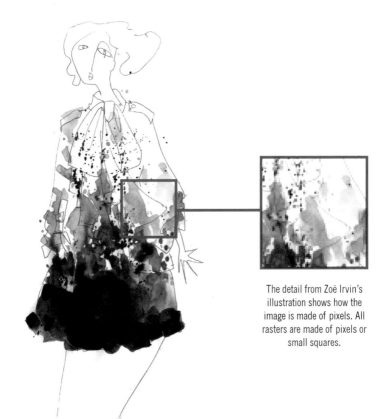

The detail from Zoë Irvin's illustration shows how the image is made of pixels. All rasters are made of pixels or small squares.

An enigmatic visual device used by illustrators and designers. A rebus means 'not by words, but by things'. It is a visual puzzle that involves the use of sounds, pictograms, symbols and signs, which replace words to reveal a message when read together. Examples can be found in the work of the Dadaists and Surrealists and in pictographic trademarks, such as Paul Rand's memorable variations on the identity for IBM and Milton Glaser's 'I ❤ New York'.

Short cuts commonly used in text messaging, such as the ones shown below, play on words and sounds much in the same way as a rebus.

L8: Late
L8r: Later
M8: Mate
ne1: Anyone

A term used in illustration to describe the use of visual material that relates to the topic or subject matter of the commission or work. Inspiration is taken from imagery created by others and elements are sometimes assimilated into the illustrator's artwork. Illustrators gather visual reference required for specific briefs from a wide range of sources. Reference imagery is substantially altered by illustrators, aware of the need to use the images to fuel their imaginations and personal visual interpretations, while not infringing on copyright.

Photography by Xavier Young

☞ see Sketchbook 215

A period of cultural movements and ideas that originated in Italy from around the 1400s and spread across the rest of Europe. Developments in the arts during this time included: linear perspective, geometry, the study of anatomy, science and nature, the invention of the printing press and the work of artists such as Giotto, Leonardo da Vinci, Michelangelo, Raphael and the German illustrator, Albrecht Dürer.

The reporting of news topics and events through the use of images.
The illustrator therefore functions as a visual journalist. The term is
related to eyewitness reporting, analysis, observation and travel.
Illustrators were in demand for periodicals such as *The Illustrated
London News* in the nineteenth century to report on people, places
and events. The illustrator has always acted as a visual journalist and
travelling documentarist.

see Drawing 86

In art, this term means the creation of recognisable, realistic or graphic depictions of subject matter and objects as they are seen in the physical world. Its opposite is abstraction or non-representational art. In illustration, it is also the manipulation of signs and visual language to communicate and stand for something else.

Representation is an important aspect of visual communication studies, aesthetics and semiotics. The works of Charles Sanders Peirce (1839–1914) and Ferdinand de Saussure (1857–1913) made a significant contribution by developing theories on iconic, symbolic and indexical representations and the theory that language is a series of signs.

Icon
An actual image of a horse, which visually represents the image being discussed.

Symbol
This horseshoe icon represents a horse at its most basic level, but it implies other meanings such as horse racing or good luck.

Index
This anvil can be associated with a horse or blacksmith, but it depicts neither.

The systematic investigation into the study of materials and sources in order to establish facts and reach new conclusions. Broad and in-depth research is the activity illustrators engage in when first receiving a brief. The act of constantly drawing and reading are also fundamental types of research.

Illustration by Amore Hirosuke

A term derived from the Latin for 'in past times' or 'backwards'. It is used to describe fashions, trends, and illustrative styles of the past. Once trends become unfashionable, they are revived or imitated in the work of illustrators in ironic and playful ways, an activity associated with Postmodernism.

☞ see Kitsch 131

An American painter and illustrator who stated that: 'I was showing the America I knew and observed to others who might not have noticed. My fundamental purpose is to interpret the typical American. I am a storyteller.' Rockwell's illustrations mirrored, described and celebrated twentieth-century America. His legacy includes the highly popular 321 covers he illustrated for *Saturday Evening Post* and his paintings on civil rights of the 1960s.

☞ see Magazines 143, Representational 197

A debated term for a movement in the arts
that emerged in the 1790s in reaction to
the Neoclassical School and the Enlightenment.
It has been seen as a precursor to Modernism
and was inspired by medievalism, folklore,
emotions and narrative. Romantic artists include
Eugene Delacroix, Théodore Géricault, the
Pre-Raphaelite Brotherhood, William Blake,
JMW Turner, Edward Bawden and
John Constable.

☛ see Arts and Crafts Movement 37

The use of wit and humour to ridicule foolish human behaviour, ideas or institutions, with an aim to improve the existing situation. For many years graphic artists have used irony, exaggeration, analogy, sarcasm and parody to make fun of and insult subjects. Examples include the witty cartoons of satirical Victorian magazines such as *Punch* and the political editorial illustrations of Steve Bell.

Image by Xavier Young

A scanner could also be used as a creative tool as it can produce interesting effects. The scanned celery above has an altered colour and produces a result that is different from a traditional photograph.

An external electronic device that digitises images by capturing, saving and converting them to digital files that can be read by the computer. Scanners have become a key tool in illustration and design; their affordability and widespread use has also impacted on the aesthetics of contemporary art practice.

☞ see Photocopier 173, Photography 174

Imaginative and fantastic stories featuring fictional projected scientific and technological developments, and their influence on people and society. The field includes travel through time and space, life on other planets, imagined technology, aliens, robots and cyborgs, and has provided illustrators with absorbing and challenging subject matter since the 1950s. Often set in the future or outer space, science fiction speculates on events, engages with a wide variety of themes and makes imaginative use of technological and scientific knowledge.

The painting below by Rowena Morill depicts the famous science-fiction author Isaac Asimov..

☞ see Fantasy 97

Illustration by Andy Potts

This is an example of a line drawing of the type commonly found in illustrators' scrapbooks. This was a personal sketch depicting inebriation.

Books with blank pages on to which items such as newspaper cuttings, postcards, illustrations, memorabilia and magazine articles are pasted down on and preserved within. Scrapbooks also exist in digital form as multimedia personal albums.

The scratching of images is associated with sgrafitto used by ceramicists on unfired clay objects, scrimshaw art images scratched on ivory or bone, or engraved on wood or metal by printmakers. Karl Angerer developed the scratchboard in 1864; it involved the use of chalk on a cardboard substrate that was covered in black ink, which was then scraped off to reveal the white clay. This technique is called 'scraperboard' in the UK and is popular with illustrators who combine line and tone with direct renderings using scalpels, old dental tools, homemade wire brushes or steel wool.

Illustration by Ceri Amphlett

☞ see Printmaking 186

Also known as 'silkscreen printing' or 'serigraphy', screen printing is a multiple printing technique and method that makes use of stencils to transfer the image. A stencil of taut finely woven fabric, such as nylon or polyester, is attached to a frame; the non-printed areas of the screen are coated or masked, the screen is then placed on the material to be printed, and a squeegee or rubber blade is used to pump ink through the areas of the screen that have not been coated.

These silk screen prints by Kate Gibb were for an exhibition entitled 'Press & Pull' held in August 2008.

☞ see Stencil 221

Illustration by James Brown

The act of advertising one's work and services.
Illustrators can promote themselves through any of
the following methods: direct mail complemented by
websites, online portfolios, social networking sites,
blogs, advertising via annuals, entering competitions and
self-initiated exhibitions. Postcards and hand-made
prints remain a popular form of self-promotion for
illustrators.

The above is an image of a two-colour screen print with copy taken from the 1960s song 'Woodstock' by
Crosby, Stills and Nash. The design process was an exercise in drawing type from memory without the aid of
a computer, in order to achieve an authentic 1960s feel.

As printing technology and publishing methods have developed, so has the imperative to 'do it yourself'. Illustrators can now take control of their creations, along with the distribution and marketing aspects of their work. Following the tradition of William Blake, William Morris, the 1960s underground press and Punk, many illustrators now engage in personal, self-initiated DIY publishing projects. Illustrators can produce limited-edition publications and merchandise and promote themselves through websites, forums, on- and off-line galleries, blogs and exhibitions.

These are copies of the self-published, mail-order newspaper *Peter Arkle News*, published since 1993 in New York City.

☞ see Authorship 40

Illustrations following on from one to another in a logical and orderly form. This term is associated with comics, graphic novels, sequential art and book illustration. Illustrators produce sequential images by editing key moments to draw; manipulating the eye's path on a picture plane; using characterisation; and establishing mood and sense of place. Sequential illustration has a long history and examples include Trajan's Column in Rome, Eygptian hieroglyphics, Greek friezes and William Hogarth's prints.

William Hogarth's engravings are an example of narrative sequential prints and paintings, and can be seen as precursors to the comic book or graphic novel.

"With proper meditation, you can get bark and bite in harmony."

The making of fortunate discoveries by chance or accident is often part of an illustrator's creative working process. The act of creating artwork using intuition, automatic drawing and found objects was a fundamental aspect of the Dada and Surrealist movements. Mistakes and so-called happy accidents are inherent in pictorial image-making such as Photoshop tweaking, silk-screen printing and life drawing, and can lead the way to new directions, visual techniques and languages.

Outline drawings, usually portraits in profile, filled in black.
The name is derived from Etienne de Silhouette (1709–1767),
a French finance minister whose name became associated with
cheaply made products. Silhouettes were a form of inexpensive
portraiture where a likeness was created from cutting paper
shadows freehand or by working from life-sized shadows
reduced by a pantograph. They first appeared in ancient
Egyptian murals and, like shadow puppets, became popular in
late sixteenth-century France.

An influential satirical magazine founded in Munich in 1896 by publisher Albert Langen and artist Thomas Theodor Heine. *Simplicissimus* combined biting satirical and political commentary with striking graphic art including works by Heine, Olaf Gulbransson, Karl Arnold, Edward Thöny and George Grosz. The illustrations in the magazine embody the publication's mix of art and satire. Attacks on society, government, clergy and the Prussian military led to prison sentences for Heine and the writer Frank Wedekind, which increased the magazine's popularity.

A board manufactured in a variety of sizes with a set of four wheels mounted below it. Skateboards feature two-metal trucks or axles, polyurethane wheels and decks, which are often illustrated by graphic artists for manufacturers. The brand identities and clothing of skate companies have also featured innovative illustrations.

Mark Wigan-designed skate and surf boards for *Fine* magazine, Japan, 1988.

☞ see Merchandising 150

Blank pads or notebooks that provide the illustrator with an essential, personal, visual-thinking tool in which to practise and experiment with mark-making and media techniques, reflect on progress, make notations, develop ideas and have fun.

It is useful to have a pocket-sized notebook to keep with you at all times as a visual diary of travels, places and events. Leonardo da Vinci, Francisco Goya, John Constable, George Grosz and Henry Moore are some of the most famous influential artists who kept sketchbooks.

These are illustrator Andy Potts's personal sketches of San Francisco and New York City.

San Francisco, downtown

new york

Illustration by Andy Potts

☞ see Scrapbooks 205

This illustration was created by Andy Potts for the American Bar Association Journal using Photoshop and scanned-in mixed-media.

Coded instructions in the form of programs, which direct the operation of computer hardware. The programs perform specific tasks such as running operating systems, utilities and applications software, which instruct the computer in processing data. The range of computer software being employed by illustrators such as Photoshop, Illustrator, Flash, Dreamweaver, Final Cut Pro and Maya provides opportunities to produce high-quality work for print, moving image and the web. New techniques are rapidly assimilated globally by digital-savvy illustrators.

A graphic convention used to convey the thoughts or words spoken by a character. Also known as a 'text bubble' or 'speech balloon', they are often used as a graphic device in comic books and were first used by illustrators in the satirical prints of the eighteenth century.

☞ see Comics 66

Often commissioned by art editors in editorial and book publishing to elucidate, amplify or interpret a story, theme or idea. Spot illustrations are usually considered to be fairly simple images one column in width.

This illustration is by A. Richard Allen, who works in the editorial illustration field for many magazines. A spot illustration is one of the ways in which his illustrations are reproduced on a magazine's pages

see Editorial Illustration 87

First introduced in Great Britain in 1840, postage stamps are square or rectangular printed labels issued by governments, to be attached to mail such as letters, postcards and packages in order to prove that the postage has been paid. Since the introduction of the world's first stamp – the Penny Black (1840) featuring an engraved portrait bust of Queen Victoria – postage stamps have proved a rewarding and challenging area of pictorial design for illustrators. Print runs for stamps can run into hundreds of millions and commissions can include popular commemorative stamps, souvenir sheets, sports events, famous people, celebrations, wildlife, architecture, art and historical events.

A renowned creator of witty and incisive drawings, whose prolific output spanned 60 years. He commented on humanity with a unique, intelligent and consistent pictorial imagination, and appropriated a wide range of artistic references. His work blurred boundaries between disciplines and included numerous covers and drawings for *The New Yorker*, as well as for books, public murals, stage-set designs and international exhibitions of sculptures, drawings, collages and prints.

☞ see Conceptual Illustration 72, New Yorker, The 158

**The reproduction of images on an underlying surface
by applying paint to areas cut into a template. The art
is related to early spray painting over hands to form
outlines in cave paintings dating before 10,000 BC.
Stencils are used to create layers in silk screen printing,
mimeography in official contexts and political, ironic and
satirical graffiti. Rapidly produced stencil street art is a
worldwide movement. Examples include the works of
anarchist punk band Crass and Banksy.**

A visual storytelling tool adopted as a way of pre-visualising live-action films from the 1940s onwards. The storyboard is now also employed in developing websites and interactive games, visual thinking in business and pitching ideas to clients. In the film industry, professional storyboard artists create two-dimensional and three-dimensional sequential illustrations to aid producers, directors, cinematographers, art directors and actors. Sergei Eisenstein, Alfred Hitchcock, the Coen Brothers and Ridley Scott are noted for their extensive use of storyboards.

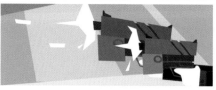

☞ see Animation 28, Sequential Illustration 210

Illustration by Janine Shroff

A form of communication aimed at recreating events that have occurred using visual, written and oral methods. Visual storytelling is an ancient cultural form of communication dating back to cave paintings. It is a fundamental aspect of illustration and is used to entertain, explain, educate and promote values through the visual interpretation of myths, legends, fables, tales and stories.

☞ see Narrative 156

Street art is a global phenomenon that infiltrates the textures of the urban environment, transforming the street into a gallery. The activity merges installation, social and political commentary, symbolic iconography, graphic logos and illustration. Examples encompass the cryptic tags of Samo, Haring's subway chalk drawings, the murals of the Bogside Artists and the 'subvertising' inspired by Adbusters.

Photography by Xavier Young

Working studios are bases to work in and run a freelance business from – they could be shared spaces or spare rooms in homes. Studios can operate as the illustrator's library or archive of visual reference material. They could also function as a museum for previously published work and serve as a gallery or showcase platform to potential clients.

☞ see Archive 33, Reference 194, Working Process 267

The distinctive features and mannerisms of an illustrator's work used to convey content, values and ideas visually. The distinctive ethos and characteristics of illustrators' and designers' work have come to define and characterise whole eras of popular and visual culture.

The images above are all portraits, but each has its own individual style.

A movement launched from Paris by André Breton in 1924 with the Manifesto of Surrealism. Influenced by Sigmund Freud's theory of the unconscious, Surrealism was concerned with interpreting dreams, free association or automatism, and was also aligned with revolutionary politics. Surrealism has had an enduring influence on illustration. Examples of surrealist artists are René Magritte, Salvador Dalí and Max Ernst.

This surreal montage is from a series of portraits (Tribu) by contemporary illustrator Catherine McIntyre.

☞ see Conceptual Illustration 72, Dada 79

The use of symbols to represent ideas or qualities. Symbolism is used to describe narrative artwork with psychological, erotic and mystical iconography and themes. Artists associated with symbolism include Edward Burne-Jones, Dante Gabriel Rossetti, Aubrey Beardsley, Paul Gauguin, Odilon Redon and Jean Delville. The use of symbols to express abstract concepts was also used extensively in surrealism.

Chris Haughton's illustration creates distinctive symbolic iconography in the form of his 'prairie dog ravers' to represent club culture for a Japanese online record store.

A term derived from the Samoan word *tatau* meaning 'to mark or strike twice'. Tattooing is the marking of the skin by pricking and filling in the punctures with indelible inks. The tattoo industry is a popular field of illustration. Interesting examples of the art include full-body Japanese yakuza and gang tattoos, Maori facial tattoos and temporary Mehndi tattoos.

☞ see Decoration 80

Images that visually communicate information relating to engineering and science, such as drawings, diagrams and charts. It can be produced for specialist users or the general public in the form of operating instructions and manuals.

Technical illustrations are required for items such as biological studies, mechanical drafting, cartography, blueprints, weather forecasts, astronomy and chemical reactions. Technical illustrators could also provide sophisticated digital imagery for museums and interactive educational products.

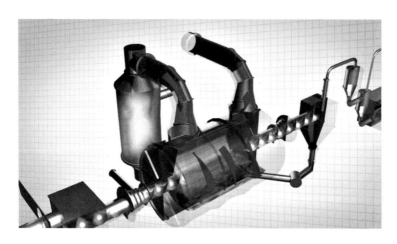

This is a still from a project by Gavin Ambrose for First London Power. It was brought to life by animation specialists, GraphixAsset Ltd. The technology is hidden so the use of fades and cutaways allows the viewer 'inside' the project.

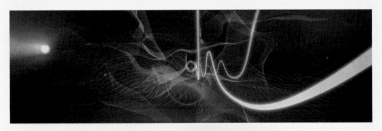

The above are animated sequences created by Andy Potts for a film about the High Speed 1 line in London and screened as part of the Royal Gala Opening of St Pancras Station in November 2007.

Images used by broadcast television for a wide range of functions including programme titles and content, especially in children's TV, channel identities, commercials, animations and set design. It is an area that makes extensive use of computer graphics, especially 3D modelling and animation.

"Retire!—What do You Think?"

An English illustrator who drew over 2000 caricatures and cartoons for *Punch* but is renowned for his distinctive illustrations engraved on blocks of wood for Lewis Carroll's best-selling children's books *Alice's Adventures in Wonderland* and *Through the Looking Glass*. The illustration above is Tenniel's 'Gladstone'.

☛ see Punch 189

WORDS AND PICTURES MANIPULATED AND JUXTAPOSED BY THE ILLUSTRATORS TO CREATE SPECIFIC MOODS OR EMOTIONS.

Illustration by Andy Potts

A PERSONAL PIECE CREATED FOR THE ONLINE GALLERY *WOODSUCH* IN RESPONSE TO A BRIEF WITH THE SAME TITLE.

☞ see Hand-drawn Type 113, Juxtaposition 129, Visual Impact 255

The use of natural or artificial fibres that have been spun to make thread, cloth or yarn and are joined by craft techniques such as weaving, knitting, sewing and crocheting. Illustrators produce images for a number of textile products including clothes, furnishings, carpets, flags, bags and towels.

☞ see Embroidery 89, Knitted Illustration 132

Pieces of art that have length, height, width and depth.
three-dimensional installations and early digitally
collaged images were pioneered in the UK in the 1980s
by English illustrators the Thunderjockeys, who studied
under the influential postmodern Dutch designer Gert
Dunbar at the Royal College of Art in London.

A tongue-in-cheek look at musical genres using three-dimensional rendering techniques,
designed by Studio Output.

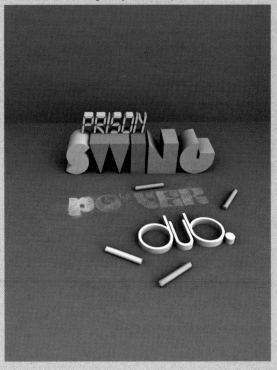

A small and quickly executed sketch that generates a number of ideas.

These images by Zoë Irvin show how quickly produced illustrations can effectively convey messages and a sense of style.

☞ see Brainstorming 51

Visual images and sounds used to present various information on a film or television programme. Title sequences include film titles, cast members and production credits. Saul Bass pioneered the development of the film title sequence as an independent art form during the 1950s and 1960s. His title sequences acted as short films containing bold and simple visual metaphors for the film's main subject matter. Sequences in films such as *The Man with the Golden Arm*, *Vertigo*, *Psycho* and *North by Northwest* are now iconic images of our visual culture.

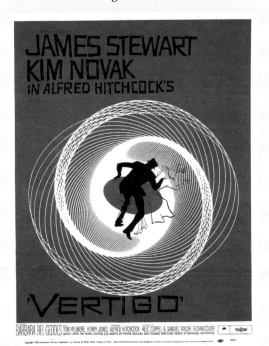

Objects that are manufactured to be played with and collected. They have ancient origins dating back to the beginning of human civilisation. Famous toys include Star Wars figures, Barbie and Lego. Many toys have been based on illustrations and vice versa.

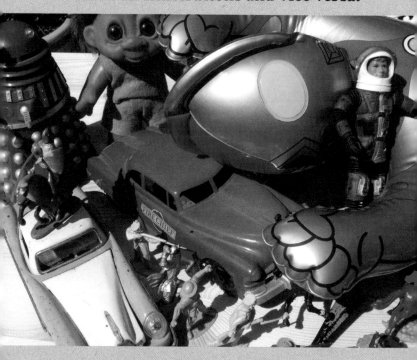

☞ See Urban Vinyl 246

Two-Step

The author found this traditional Victorian postcard from a flea market.

An illustration that places emphasis on looking, thinking, seeing and observing. Traditional illustrations include personal and hand-crafted techniques used by illustrators. Diverse approaches include animation, silk-screen, embroidery, collage and three-dimensional work.

☛ see Victorian Illustration 250

An illustration that records or documents natural history, cartography and the customs and cultures of indigenous peoples. Artists such as John Webber, José Cardero, Ludovik Choris and Jonathan Carver observed how people lived and conveyed the atmosphere of their surroundings. Technical advances in all forms of transport have also provided illustrators with a rich source of travel subject matter, from the picturesque tourist books of the nineteenth century to the Golden Age of travel posters during the 1920s and 1930s.

The above images are personal travel pieces created by
Andy Potts and Tim Marrs in April 2007.

☞ see Reportage 196

The general direction in which illustration moves – a prevailing style that can be recorded historically and followed by illustrators. As it is easier for some illustrators to copy than to think of something new, many follow the latest trend. Clients look for a version of the next big thing and young illustrators desire to be part of the latest 'cool' movement and join others who seek to differentiate their work from other traditions or visual styles. Trends have included mimicking the work of modern art movements and outsider art, and imitating the work of illustrators from the 1940s and 1950s.

This mini world was created by Studio Output using hand-drawn illustrations for a student pack for London-based club, Ministry of Sound.

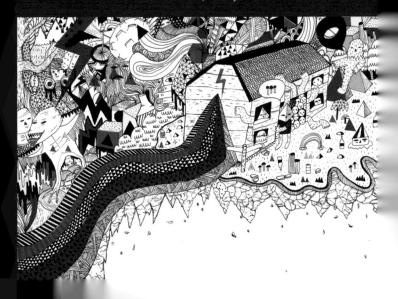

French for 'fool the eye', it is an optical illusion created by producing a detailed two-dimensional image and making it appear three dimensional, thereby deceiving the viewer into thinking that they are seeing an actual object. Often rendered on walls as decorative effects, trompe l'oeil uses light and shadow to create depth and trick the viewer with naturalistic detail.

T-shirt by Duffer St George

The T-shirt is thought to have originated as a garment worn by the British and American navies in the early twentieth century. T-shirts were worn by the US Army and Navy during the Second World War. T-shirts were popularised in the 1950s by Marlon Brando in films such as *A Street Car Named Desire* and *The Wild One*, and James Dean in *Rebel Without a Cause*. T-shirts are used by artists and illustrators to exhibit their works and they remain iconic forms of visual communication.

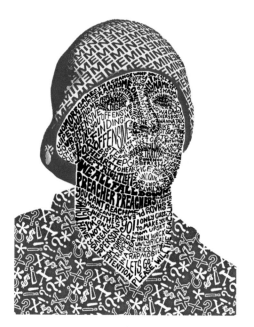

Illustration by James Brown

Refers to the style and appearance of printed matter. Many illustrators collaborate with designers who commission work and apply typefaces on to artwork for reproduction. Typography and typeface design can now be generated by illustrators using software and computers. Typography is a constantly-evolving discipline that conveys messages through the use of design and the selection and composition of typefaces.

This is a portrait of the rapper Eminem commissioned by *GQ* magazine.
His face comprises of lyrics to his songs, while his hoody is made with the symbols
'x@*!X?' to represent the obscenities in his lyrics.

☞ See Hand-drawn Type 113, Text and Image 233

A GENRE OF ARTWORK PRODUCED IN JAPAN BETWEEN THE SEVENTEENTH AND TWENTIETH CENTURIES. THE PRINTS FEATURE FLAT, BOLD COLOURS, THE RHYTHMIC AND SENSUOUS USE OF LINE AND ASYMMETRICAL COMPOSITION. SUBJECT MATTER RANGES FROM KABUKI THEATRE, SUMO WRESTLERS, COURTESANS, NATURE AND HISTORICAL TALES TO EROTICA. LEADING ARTISTS INCLUDE HOKUSAI, HIROSHIGE, MORONOBU, KUNIYOSHI, UTAMARO AND MASANOBU.

This work by Hokusai is entitled 'Behind the Great Wave of Kanagawa' (1823–1829).

☞ see Woodcut 265

Highly collectable casts of characters and limited edition series of vinyl figures. Urban vinyl has provided a new outlet for the imaginations of illustrators and designers in the twenty-first century. Hand-made, limited-edition designer soft toys by the likes of Devil Robots, Boris Hopek and Pretty Ugly are popular with adult collectors.

The products below are vinyl toys made by Devil Robots in Japan.

☞ see Toys 238

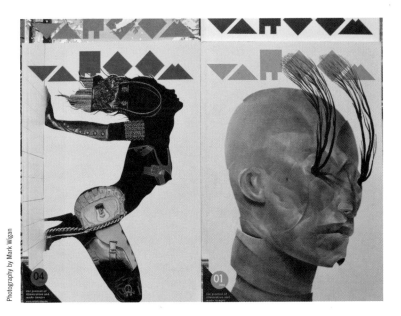

Photography by Mark Wigan

The journal of illustration and images published three times a year by the *Association of Illustrators*. The publication was launched in 2006 and investigates the work of practitioners from around the world, who are making significant contributions to illustration and image-making. Writers, commentators and illustrators are given a platform to discuss illustration in a wider context, and image-makers and schools from the past are referenced.

☞ see Organisations 161

AN IMAGE CREATED USING MATHEMATICAL COORDINATES. PUT SIMPLY, IN ORDER TO CREATE A LINE, ALL YOU NEED TO KNOW IS THE START POINT AND THE END POINT. TO CREATE AN ARCH, YOU NEED THE START POINT, THE END POINT AND THE ANGLE, OR TRAJECTORY, OF THE LINE. UNLIKE A RASTER IMAGE, A VECTOR CAN BE SCALED, WITHOUT ANY DEGRADATION OF QUALITY.

The vector image (top, left) and its detail, show how enlarging does not degrade quality. The vector is made of mathematical points and is scalable. The raster image (above, left) however, degrades when enlarged as it is made of squares or pixels. These elements begin to show up (as seen in the raster detail) when the enlargement is too great.

see Line 137, Raster 192

The characteristic visual languages of specific groups, countries and regions. It usually covers popular imagery often adapted from a formal style, which also sometimes derives influence from folk traditions.

An eclectic mix of ornaments and vernacular art could serve as inspiration to an illustrator.

"Mama, shall I have beautiful long hair like you when I grow up?"
"Certainly, my dear, if you use **'Edwards' Harlene'**."

An advert from the Victorian era taken from the author's archive of printed ephemera.

ILLUSTRATION CREATED DURING THE REIGN OF
QUEEN VICTORIA OF GREAT BRITAIN (1837–1901).
DURING QUEEN VICTORIA'S REIGN, THOUSANDS OF
ILLUSTRATED BOOKS AND PERIODICALS WERE PUBLISHED.
THE VICTORIAN PERIOD EMBODIED TECHNICAL INVENTION
AND EXPERIMENTATION, RESULTING IN ADVANCES IN
PHOTOGRAPHY AND PRINTING PROCESSESES.

An area that reflects contemporary illustrators' continuing search to find new audiences and outlets for their imagery. Club culture has always provided exciting opportunities to provide cross-media cultural interventions. Video jockey hardware and software continue to evolve from early film loops and slide projections to fractal generation programs, vision mixers and DVD players for scratching real-time video playback.

One of Addictive TV's international audio-visual events.

A section of *The Beethoven Frieze* (1902) by Austrian painter, illustrator and co-founder of the Vienna Secession, Gustav Klimt. Klimt is renowned for his decorative and erotic images of the female body.

A GROUP FORMED BY YOUNG ARTISTS WHO BROKE AWAY FROM OFFICIAL ACADEMIES AND ASSOCIATIONS. THE VIENNA SECESSION WAS FOUNDED IN APRIL 1897 AND LED BY SYMBOLIST PAINTER, GUSTAV KLIMT. THE GROUP'S AIMS ALIGNED WITH THE GERMAN JUGENDSTIL AND THE ART NOUVEAU MOVEMENT, EMPHASISING ARCHITECTURE, INTERIORS AND DECORATIVE, FLAT, GEOMETRIC DESIGN.

☞ see Art Nouveau 36, Decoration 80, Psychedelic 187

Illustration by George Cruikshank courtesy of www.CartoonStock.com

An illustration that has the background or
border shaded or faded at the edges, which in
turn highlights the centre of the image. Examples
include the hundreds of finely detailed, wood-
engraved book illustrations by Thomas Bewick
and the output of the Dalziel Brothers – skilful
commercial engravers, who reproduced drawings
by other illustrators including George du
Maurier, John Tenniel and John Everett Millais.

☞ see Bewick, Thomas 45, Tenniel, Sir John 232

'Second Life' illustration by Paul Sermon

// SIMULATED AND COMPUTER-BASED ENVIRONMENTS. THEY INCLUDE A MYRIAD OF FORMS, FROM INSTANT MESSAGING AND VIRTUAL FORUMS TO BLOGS AND 3D GAMES. OFTEN ACCESSED BY MULTIPLE USERS, COMPUTER-SIMULATED, 3D VIRTUAL WORLDS ALLOW USERS TO INTERACT WITH ONE ANOTHER VIA AVATARS. THE TALENTS OF ILLUSTRATORS ARE EMPLOYED IN DESIGNING MODELLED FANTASY WORLDS AND CHARACTERS FOR VIRTUAL WORLDS, SUCH AS WORLD OF WARCRAFT AND SECOND LIFE.//

☞ see Computer-generated Imagery (CGI) 71

An immediate and powerful visual impression that can influence and affect people to change their behaviour. Items such as posters can combine the creative imagination of the artist with strong ideas and design skills in order to persuade, inform, educate or protest.

'Capital Expense' by Peter Kennard

Stag Resonate, one of a series of animals beautifully and meticulously illustrated in sinuous line.

Illustration by Si Scott

The use of visual images to communicate ideas, which are the representation of an illustrator's concepts. Illustrators convey ideas and messages and solve problems through distinct and personal visual languages. The emotions, feelings and behaviour of the viewer are manipulated through numerous creative possibilities and the use of symbolism, exaggeration, visual metaphors, similes and juxtapositions. Developing a personal visual language involves incessant practice, research and an acute awareness of context and the target audience.

The word 'metaphor' is derived from the Greek 'to carry over or across'. An item or idea is moved in place of something else, and therefore context becomes key. Illustrators can play with signs, ambiguous meanings and visual allusions to create coherence through the use of metaphor. Visual metaphors draw comparisons and connections between items that are distinctly different, in order to convey an idea.

'Suburban Bliss' by Izzie Klingels

☞ see Ideas 120, Juxtaposition 129

An illustration by a visual reporter who travelled to combat zones worldwide, sending back illustrations to the *Illustrated London News*.

Stop (2005) by Peter Kennard is one of many protest images produced against the invasion of and conflict in Iraq.

Images produced during the nineteenth century by illustrators known as 'Special Artists'. These illustrators worked worldwide on assignments as eye-witness visual journalists recording wars, disasters and expeditions for periodicals. During the First and Second World Wars, Britain initiated the official 'War Artists' Scheme' to record for posterity wars involving Britain. This led to impressive works by artists such as Wyndham Lewis, CRW Nevinson, Paul Nash and Eric Ravilious.

An enduring painting medium used extensively
throughout the history of illustration. Watercolour is
commonly used in the botanical and wildlife field to
represent nature. The medium became very popular in
England during the eighteenth and nineteenth centuries
for capturing topographical studies, picturesque
landscapes and journeys. The continued popularity of
watercolour can be seen in the use of washes and glazes in
contemporary natural history and fashion illustration.

'Scottish Seascape' by Nick Herbert

☞ see Paint 165

Internet platforms that act as showcases for illustrators. Websites need to be regularly updated and easy to navigate. They present biographical information about artists and their works; provide portfolios, and supply contact and exhibition details. Art directors usually commission by browsing websites.

These are collage frameworks comprising real objects and cardboard models, representing specific programmes and campaigns. Constructed by hand, the collages suggest the creative flair of the network. Online, the stills come to life.

Designed and illustrated by NB Studio

☛ **See Art Director 35**

A classic, best-selling children's picture book originally published in 1963 by Harper & Row. It was drawn and written by the renowned illustrator and author Maurice Sendak. The adventures of Max and his meetings with imaginary, mythical creatures have become accepted as one of the most important and best-loved examples of children's literature. The book has been honoured with a number of awards, including the prestigious Caldecott Medal in 1964 and continues to beguile and enchant children to this day.

☞ see Children's Books 61

'Dog's Dinner' by Peter Field

DOG'S   DINNER.

Illustrations that are odd, capricious, amusing,
fantastic and peculiar. A substantial number of
illustrations published over the centuries can be
described using this term. Some of the works of
Edward Lear, Sir John Tenniel, Randolph Caldecott,
Dr Seuss and Quentin Blake can be classified
as whimsical illustration.

A useful medium and platform for illustrators to showcase their work. Store windows around the world often feature live painting events and work by graphic artists (as seen below) to seduce shoppers through their doors.

A mental faculty incorporating speed of perception and the association of incongruous and unrelated elements. In illustration, wit can effectively evoke humour or surprise. The extensive use of visual verbal puns and substituting of one image for another can be seen in the inventive and memorable work of artists such as Charles Philipon, Saul Steinberg and Milton Glaser.

This work by Craig Atkinson displays wit by juxtaposing images that would not normally be associated with one another in order to spark a new and humorous association in the viewer's mind.

see Humour 118

The oldest form of relief printing, in which the image is carved parallel with the wood-grain. The raised parts of the design carry the ink, and the parts not to be printed are cut away with tools such as a knife or gouge. Outstanding examples include the Japanese Ukiyo-e school of woodcuts by artists such as Hiroshige and Hokusai.

This is an image of Albrecht Dürer's woodcut, *The Revelation of St John: The Four Riders of the Apocalypse* (1497–1498).

☛ see Ukiyo-e 245, Wood Engraving 266

A process in which the image is incised on to the edge grain of the wood, producing finer lines than woodcuts. This form of engraving became the most popular way of printing for the growing publications market in the nineteenth century. Illustrations were cut on to the wooden blocks by professional engravers and then printed rapidly on the new steam presses. English wood engraver Thomas Bewick pioneered the technique in the 1790s.

☞ see Bewick, Thomas 45, Printmaking 186

A distinctive series of actions taken by the illustrator in order to produce images. There is no formula for image-making, as every illustrator solves visual problems with their own unique working process, while manipulating techniques and tools with skill and imagination. Picture-making calls for original ways of thinking and experimentation with ideas, form, colour and composition.

The working methods of various artists:

'Pencil for thoughts, ink for decision. White sheet of paper for a clear mind. State of stillness'.

Ian Pollock

'Notebook after notebook after notebook, because I feel sick when I forget potentially good ideas. I don't slack, I take photographs, I draw, I scan, I Photoshop.'

'It usually starts with walking around my house looking in books, followed by a cup of tea. Then some shambolic fumbling with roller printing ink and scanner. Lastly, an attempt to orchestrate everything on computer.'

Sarah Jones

☞ see Ideas 120

A quarterly, literary periodical published in the late nineteenth century by Charles Elkin Mathews and John Lane in London. *The Yellow Book* featured illustrations, short stories, essays and poetry. This highly influential and trend-setting periodical symbolised English aestheticism and the decadent zeitgeist of its day. Fin de siècle illustrator, Aubrey Beardsley, art directed early volumes of the publication and designed posters in order to advertise the book.

...bmarine

...eature-length musical directe...
...g and animated by Heinz Edel...
...1968 featuring the music o...
...epper's Lonely Hearts Club B...
...ty of animation techniques...
...ction and rotoscoping. The...
...edelia, pop art and 1960s...

A German word derived from *zeit* meaning 'time' and *geist* meaning 'spirit'. Literally, it means 'spirit of the age'. The twenty-first century zeitgeist covers topics such as consumerism, nostalgia, celebrity culture and global warming. Anti-corporate statements, social networking sites, hand-crafted images and collectives are all part of the zeitgeist.

☞ see Style 226, Trends 241

Photocopied and self-published publications that cover a wide range of subjects and have small circulations aimed at specific readers. They derive from the tradition of self-published, political pamphlets and chapbooks, science-fiction fanzines, comics and the 1960s underground press. Many personal zines have evolved into websites and blogs, although printed zines remain popular with their own international distribution networks.

The Details

30,000 BC
Cave Paintings
The evolution of illustration mirrors the rise of civilisation itself. Paintings discovered on the walls and ceilings of caves in Altamira, Spain, and Lascaux, France, visually communicate scenes from life, but their exact function remains a mystery. Large animals portrayed amid human handprints and abstract forms could have been created to fulfil ritual, decorative or informational objectives.

3500 BC
Sumerian Clay Tablets
Tools such as chisels, reeds and styluses were invented for carving and inscribing messages on to wax and clay tablets, stone, wood and papyrus. The Sumerians used cuneiform – the world's oldest logographic writing system. Pictograms were used in the schematic clay tokens of China and the codices of the Mayans and Aztecs.

3200 BC
Hieroglyphics
From the Greek word *hiero* meaning 'sacred', ancient Egyptian hieroglyphics integrated phonetic and pictographic signs with abstract and observational images. Symbolic conventions such as heads depicted in profile, torsos viewed from the front, and legs in three-quarter view are evident in illustrated scrolls such as the *Book of the Dead* and the *Ramesseum Papyrus*.

AD 700
Illuminated Manuscripts
Tablets and papyrus scrolls were gradually replaced by vellum and the introduction of the codex from the first century AD. Ornate Books of Hours and Psalters were made in monasteries and illuminated with pigments in egg tempera and gold to symbolically represent the sacred texts. Highly decorated examples include the *Gospels of Lindisfarne* c698 AD and the *Book of Kells* c800 AD. The latter is noted for interlacing swirls and ornate initials and borders.

1435
Perspective
The introduction and development of perspective systems and aids for drawing during the Renaissance advanced illustration in technical, scientific, architectural and medicinal fields.
The theories of the linear perspective inventor, Filippo Brunelleschi, and the writings of Leon Battista Alberti made a significant contribution to the ordering of space and naturalism through the direct observation of nature.

1450s
Block Books
Crude and cheap illustrated woodcut books and broadsheets were printed in Germany and the Netherlands in the fifteenth century from engraved wooden blocks. The technique had been pioneered in China in the ninth century AD and there are many examples of coloured block books printed in China and Japan.

1452
Intaglio
The printing technique introduced in the fifteenth century that involves the printing of images from recessed lines and tonal areas incised into the surface of a copper, zinc or stone plate. Intaglio processes include etching, engraving, aquatint, mezzotint and soft ground. The plates are smeared with ink, which enters the depressed areas. The surface is then wiped clean and an etching press is used to transfer the ink on to the paper. The technique was later popularised by Jacques Callot and Rembrandt.

1498
Albrecht Dürer
German painter, print maker and theorist generally regarded as the most significant and influential artist of the Northern European Renaissance. His popular and detailed graphic work extended the field of woodcut and engraved printmaking. Important works include the Apocalypse woodcuts of 1498 and his copper plate etchings such as *Knight, Death and the Devil, Melancholia* (1514) and the *Rhinoceros* woodcut of 1515.

1633
Jacques Callot
A prolific printmaker born in Lorraine in 1592, who chronicled his times with over a thousand highly detailed etchings. Using sharp, incisive lines and excellent technique, Callot's prints recorded court scenes for the Medici family and captured the lives of gypsies, soldiers, beggars and courtiers. His powerful Miseries and Misfortunes of War prints from 1633 exposed the inhumanity of conflict and would later inspire the work of Goya.

1680s
Ukiyo-e
Japanese wood-block prints produced in metropolitan Edo, Tokyo, between the seventeenth and twentieth centuries, which focused on the 'floating world'. The flat colours, sensuous lines and asymmetrical compositions of artists such as Moronobu (1618–1694), Hokusai (1760–1849) and Hiroshige (1797–1849) had an enduring influence on European artists and illustrators.

1731
William Hogarth
One of the most important eighteenth-century British artists credited with inventing the use of sequential prints that would later become the precursor to the comic strip. Hogarth's sequential paintings and engravings – *Harlot's Progress* (1731) and *A Rake's Progress* (1735) feature moral warnings and a satirical and critical attitude to society. Hogarth's engravings were sold through print shops and the copying of his work led to his campaign for the introduction of the Copyright Act of 1735.

1796
Lithography
The invention of lithography, credited to the German Alois Senefelder in 1796, transformed the art of illustration. It was the first flat surface, planographic, printing process and was based on the principle that oil and water do not mix. Delacroix, Toulouse-Lautrec, Daumier and Bonnard made imaginative use of the process, drawing with oily ink or litho crayon on flat lithographic stones.

1790s
Wood Engraving
A process that achieved finer line detail than woodcuts by incising the image across the dense end grain of box wood. The technique was revolutionised by Thomas Bewick in the 1790s in his beautiful and accurate books such as *History of British Birds*, volumes one and two. The process proved popular with professional illustrators and engravers of the nineteenth century and was used for the expanding books and periodicals markets.

1800s
Goya
Spanish court painter and printmaker considered by some to be the father of modern art. His highly influential output included the groundbreaking paintings *Naked Maya* and *Clothed Maya* c1800-1805, the satirical and macabre etchings *Los Caprichos* and his horrific depictions of the atrocities of war in the *Disasters of War* engravings (1810–1814), printed after his death in 1863.

1850s
Honoré Daumier
French painter, sculptor and professional illustrator born in 1808, who drew over 4000 lithographs, many of which caricatured and ridiculed bourgeois society in Paris. His satirical illustrations for *La Caricature* of King Louis Philippe as a gluttonous Gargantua led to a prison sentence. An exceptional visual journalist, his graphic work also appeared in the influential *Le Charivari*.

1850s
The Industrial Revolution

The socio-economic changes that first took place in Britain between 1750 and 1850 affected the whole world. The rapid growth of large-scale capitalism, extensive mechanisation of production, specialisation and urban factory production led to a demand for all kinds of printed material. This demand was aided by inventions such as photography, steam-powered presses, chromolithography, half-tone screens and photogravure. The new town and city dwellers required pictorial information and the profession of illustration answered that need.

1860s
The Golden Age

The 1860s are described as the Golden Age of British professional illustration. This period saw developments in print technology and the publication and distribution of affordable books and periodicals. The demand for graphic journalism and information saw Cruikshank, Keene, Doyle, Homer and Tenniel become household names for their work in periodicals. Pre-Raphaelite painters and illustrators, such as Dante Gabriel Rossetti and John Everett Millais, drew elaborate pen-and-ink work, which was reproduced by the engravers the Dalziel Brothers.

1880s
Arts and Crafts Movement

Emerged in Britain in response to the effects of the social conditions and poor design produced during the Industrial Revolution. The movement was pioneered by William Morris, who emphasised the integrity of materials and the fusing of fine and applied arts, craftsmanship and functional design. He also launched the Kelmscott Press in 1891 to produce limited edition books inspired by revivals of historicist styles and small-scale medieval printing. Ideas from this movement were adopted internationally and led to the modernist movement.

1890s'
Art Nouveau

An international movement in art, architecture, products, graphics and illustration, which literally means 'new art' in French. The movement contributed to the break with neoclassical historicism and the transition to twentieth-century Modernism. Jules Cheret and Alphonse Mucha exemplify the distinctive visual style of the movement with whiplash curves, asymmetrical letterforms and undulating lines.

1890s
Poster Art

During the late nineteenth century, commercial artists, such as Jules Cheret, Eugene Grasset, Henri de Toulouse-Lautrec and Alphonse Mucha reached large audiences with their vibrant, lithographic posters, which eventually became highly collectable. Industrialisation led to advertising displays and posters becoming a form of public art, which caused debates over the ownership of public space.

1898
Illustrators Members' Clubs

In England, illustrators known as black-and-white artists became members of clubs such as the Artists' Society in the 1820s. The London Sketch Club was established in 1898 as a social haven for leading graphic artists of its day and formed two distinct groups: fairy illustrators and poster illustrators. In 1901, the Society of Illustrators was founded in New York to promote the art of illustration and hold exhibitions.

1905
Children's Books
The period from 1905 to the 1930s is regarded as the Golden Age of children's book illustrations. Benchmarks were set by George Cruikshank, Sir John Tenniel, Randolph Caldecott and Kate Greenaway. Beautiful colour plate illustrations inspired by Romanticism, fables and folk tales served as a reaction to industrialisation.

1912
Expressionist Illustration
Powerful book illustration evident in the work of the Die Brücke group (1905–1913), which included Oskar Kokoschka and Ernst Ludwig Kirchner, and the raw commentaries of Käthe Kollwitz, Otto Dix, Max Beckmann and George Grosz. The images reflected a time of social and economic upheaval and revolution in Europe, a rejection of bourgeois values and horror at the machine-made mass slaughter of the First World War.

1916
Dada
A movement that served as protest against The First World War. Tristan Tzara formed the anarchic Dada movement in neutral Switzerland in 1916, and it spread to Paris, Berlin and New York. Works from this period are characterised by biting satire, anti-art shock tactics, the introduction of chance and photomontage. Artists such as George Grosz, John Heartfield and Hannah Höch created a powerful graphic language that appropriated commercial images and was later itself assimilated by the advertising industry for its commercial aims.

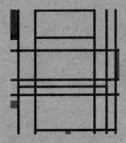

1910
The Modern Movement
Ideas such as the need for social change, collaboration with industry and form following function were disseminated by the Arts and Crafts Movement, Art Nouveau, Viennese Design and Aestheticism. Avant-garde designers assimilated Futurism and Dada and felt that through formal experimentation, abstraction and functionalism, design would radically change society. Modern design as a discipline arrived in 1919 with the founding of the Bauhaus in Weimar.

1919
Constructivism
Born out of the Soviet revolution and the desire to change society, artists and designers including Alexander Rodchenko, El Lissitzky, Vladimir Tatlin, Vladimir Mayakovsky and the Stenberg Brothers used bold typography, dynamic formal graphic languages, photomontage and geometric forms while embracing technology. Constructivists advertised products, created sets for theatre and cinema, and created graphic design, fashion design, industrial design and architecture.

1925
Art Deco
Characterised by glamour, simplicity, geometric motifs, zig-zags, bold colours and streamlined forms. It affected design from the 1920s to the 1940s. Art Deco appeared in architecture, children's books, furnishings, textiles, fashion designs, set designs and all sorts of printed matter. The poster designs of Edward McKnight Kauffer, A M Cassandre and Jean Carlu exemplify the spirit and idealism of the style.

1930
Newspaper Comics

A genre pioneered by
Rodolphe Töpffer in 1830
and extended by R F
Outcault in the 1890s.
Syndicated newspaper
comics boomed in the
1920s and the 1930s.
Benchmarks in the
field included Winsor
McCay's *Little Nemo in
Slumberland*, Frank King's
Gasoline Alley, Rockwell
Chester Gould's *Dick Tracy*,
Alex Raymond's *Flash
Gordon* and Hergé's *Tin Tin*.

1940
Wartime Propaganda

During the Second World
War, rhetorical illustration
was employed to persuade
and influence the behaviour
of large numbers of people.
Systematic political
advertising campaigns
featured national
stereotypes and symbols
such as the hammer and
sickle, swastikas, heroic
soldiers, workers and
national flags. Photography
and painted illustration
were employed to promote
causes. Striking posters
were created by Norman
Rockwell, Ben Shahn,
Abram Games and
Jean Carlu.

1945
Norman Rockwell

Popular and prolific
American illustrator who
created over 4000 original
works romanticising
America. He illustrated
40 books and is most
renowned for his
remarkable 321 covers for
the *Saturday Evening
Post*. Working in a painted
representational style, he
stated that his fundamental
purpose was to interpret the
typical American.

1950
English Neo-Romanticism
Between the wars and after
the Second World War,
English illustrators fused
Modernism with an English
Romantic tradition that
echoed the era of Samuel
Palmer and William Blake.
Despite post-war austerity,
book illustration and
publicity poster design
flourished, thanks to the
talents of illustrators such
as Eric Ravilious, Edward
Bawden, John Piper and
Mervyn Peake.

1960
Conceptual Illustration
From the mid 1950s, art
directors and designers
collaborated with
illustrators in the era of
the 'big idea' approach to
design. Magazines covered
more complex social and
cultural themes, and
illustrators moved away
from the representational
approach by choosing
to embrace conceptual
thinking, wit, metaphor
and illusion. Conceptual
illustrators, such as Saul
Steinberg and Paul Davis
appropriated ideas from
Expressionism and
Surrealism for their
commentaries.

1968
Counter Culture
In the 1960s, a non-
conformist youth movement
arose that was associated
with sex, drugs, rock 'n'
roll and anti-war and anti-
consumerist politics.
Illustration became an
integral expressive feature
of the counter culture.
Iconic imagery of the period
includes Milton Glaser's
Dylan poster, *Oz* magazine,
the comics of Robert
Crumb, Peter Blake's
artwork for The Beatles and
the psychedelic posters of
Wes Wilson and Victor
Moscoso.

1976
Postmodernism

A reaction to Modernism's universality and the principles of corporate international graphic design, Postmodernism is eclectic, decorative, retro, ironic and playful. The approach was pioneered by the output of Push Pin Studios in New York, Memphis Design, Punk and New Wave record sleeves, zines, alternative comics and political activist graphics. From the 1970s onwards, historical styles were appropriated and synthesised into pastiche as many image makers emphasised expression and ornamentation over simplicity.

1984
New Wave Illustration

The 1980s began with the launch of Art Spiegelman's and Françoise Mouly's *RAW Magazine* – an influential showcase of narrative illustration and comic art. The decade featured the publication of a vibrant and eclectic new wave of graphic art. Notable contributions were made by Ralph Steadman, Steve Bell, Donna Muir, Sue Huntley, Brian Grimwood and Raymond Briggs. 1984 saw the launch of the Apple Macintosh – a development that would profoundly impact on illustrators of the next decade.

2008
Digital Revolution

Technological developments and the World Wide Web have transformed the practice and business of illustration. The distinctive and personal visual languages of illustrators continue to be in demand, while reflecting and interpreting our age of anxiety. This is evident in DIY authorial projects, graphic novels, children's books, branding, political activism, fashion, information design, music graphics, interactive media and editorial commentary.

Conclusion

This book acts as a comprehensive resource for anyone interested in the art and craft of illustration by providing a reference to the many terms associated with the discipline. It also provides an insight into the development of a constantly evolving profession and its relationships and synergies with art and design movements, cultural contexts and technical advances. Illustration is an ancient applied art form; a powerful, life-affirming and beguiling form of contemporary visual communication. Its history is inseparable from the history of civilisation itself and it will continue to play a vital role in illuminating human experience in the future.

Illustration by Anthony Fournier

I would like to thank all those who supported me during the writing of this book and the many leading contemporary illustrators from all over the world who allowed the reproduction of their images. Thanks are due to all illustrators, past and present, for their inspiration and contributions to the expanding field of illustration. Thank you also to Gavin Ambrose for the design of the book and a final thank you to Brian Morris, Renée Last and Caroline Walmsley at AVA Publishing for their patience and support throughout the making of this miniature magnus opus.

While this volume is by no means exhaustive, we have tried our best to include all those terms that are most commonly used in the realm of illustration. If you feel that we have missed any entries then please do let us know by sending us an email marked Visual Dictionary of Illustration Entries to: enquiries@avabooks.co.uk. Please include your name and address, and if your entry makes it to an updated later edition of the book, we will send you a copy for free!

Index of Synonyms and   288
Cross References